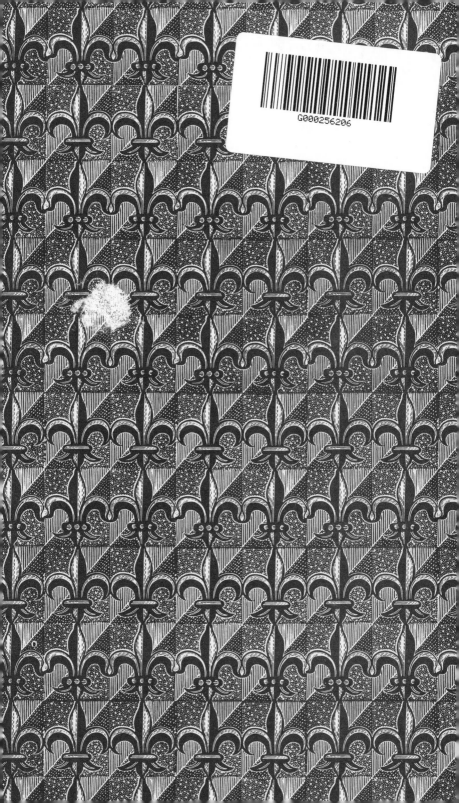

# A PLACE IN ITALY

# SIMON MAWER

# *A Place in Italy*

SINCLAIR-STEVENSON

First published in Great Britain by
Sinclair-Stevenson
7/8 Kendrick Mews
London SW7 3HG England

Copyright © 1992 by Simon Mawer
Illustrations copyright © 1992 by Clive Birch

British Library Cataloguing in Publication Data
A CIP catalogue record for this book is available from the British Library.

ISBN: 1 85619 177 X

Typeset by Rowland Phototypesetting Ltd
Bury St Edmunds, Suffolk

Printed and bound in Great Britain by
Butler & Tanner Ltd, Frome and London

*For Matthew*

# Acknowledgements

I would like to thank Avvocato Riccardo dalla Vedova for his interest and advice; Clive Birch for his elegant and evocative drawings; and of course my wife, who plays such a large part in this book and who has always shared my love of Italy.

# 1

We came in the heat of summer, in August, and found the city deserted by its inhabitants, devoid even of the Holy Father who had fled for the relative cool of the Alban hills. Shops were closed, museums were closed, landlords had gone away. The modern Romans had abandoned *piazza*, *via* and *vicolo* to a rabble army which wandered the cobbles, cameras at the ready, in search of any inhabitant who might have had the temerity to stay behind. It had the look of a scorched-earth policy employed by a citizens' army. The familiar sights – Colosseum, Pantheon, Castel Sant' Angelo, Saint Peter's – lay supine beneath the sun and the assault of the invaders.

'You shouldn't have come so early,' Natale told us gloomily. 'Everyone's out of town. You can't find *anything* at this time of year.' *Natale*, Christmas. He was the one to help us find accommodation. He was stout and genial and Calabrese, with a command of English born on the other side of the Atlantic.

'But we were *told* to come this early.'

A shake of the head. 'Not at *Ferragosto*.'

*Ferragosto*: the mid-August holiday of Santa Maria Assunta. A word of curious etymology but, for any Italian, pregnant with meaning. The beach. Idleness. Food and sleep. *Dolce far niente*. Shuttered shops and shuttered cities and damn the people left behind, *poveri bastardi*.

'Do you remember that *Ferragosto* when we were on duty at Fregene?' – a doctor reminiscing in a hospital bar one summer's afternoon years later – 'Do you remember the crowds on the beach?'

'They were bringing them in by the score,' his colleague recalled. 'Fourteen drowned.' They roared with laughter.

'Like . . . What are those animals? In Norway.'

'*Arvicole*.'

'No, you find *arvicole* here.'

A debate ensued but no one knew the name except me, and then really only in English or in the ancestor of their own language in the only living function left to it: *Lemmus lemmus*. Lemming. They were drowning like lemmings that *Ferragosto*. Surely it is a potent word to the Italians. Pavese even named a collection of short stories for it: *Feria d'Agosto*.

After the holiday, as tradition demands, the weather broke. We played scrabble and backgammon in our *pensione* while beyond the windows rain poured down in a flood of almost tropical proportions. Then, just as abruptly, the storms passed, leaving the outskirts of Rome like a suburb of Hades, bereft of inhabitants, bereft of tourists, steaming in renewed heat.

'People will start coming back, you'll see,' Natale assured us, serving us summer pasta, which was cold spaghetti with chopped *basilico* and fresh tomatoes and *mozzarella*. 'You must have patience.' *Pazienza*. Oh, you need that. Rome is a city of some three and a half million people but that year there seemed to be only about five places to let at anything we might afford. We wandered dispiriting suburbs for days on end and saw nothing. We scanned the accommodation pages of the newspaper in vain.

*AAAAAAFFITTASI. VILLA, CINQUE CAMERE, DOPPI SERVIZI, GIARDINO, MANSARDA CON SERVIZI. PREZZO ASTRONOMICO.*

One of our few hopes was on the Via Salaria, the salt road which led the legions out through the Apennine mountains to Venice but which led us nowhere that day. The landlady viewed us with suspicion. I could imagine her in Southend or Black-pool, looking sideways for a glimpse of the wedding ring. No swimming things indoors, towels not to be taken on the beach, sand to be kept outside. At all costs, that. And children? We had no children. Just the two of us, and two suitcases.

It seemed that we had come to some kind of agreement but soon after we got back to our *pensione* Natale phoned. 'She says it's not for rent any longer.'

'Someone else has taken it? But you said she said –'

'She says she's not renting it after all. She wants it for her daughter.'

'Like hell she does. She's got a typed list of Rules and Regulations on the kitchen wall, like a bloody Brighton' – generous in the extreme – 'bedsit.'

'Bloody what?'

'It doesn't matter.'

'There was something else. She seemed to think that C . . . That dress she was wearing . . .' A pregnant pause. 'She's not expecting, is she?'

STRICTLY NO CHILDREN: the unwritten clause in Rules and Regulations. There is always an unwritten rule.

'I'll take her for a pregnancy test,' I suggested, only half in jest. But even scientific evidence would have failed to per-suade. No Roman is going to reverse an idea conceived in prejudice. And it was a seller's market.

\*

In the event, after fruitless weeks of searching, we came up with this: *AVEA CENTRO STORICO. PER AFFITTO. BICAMERA CON SERVIZI, CUCINA.*

'Avea?' Natale grimaced. 'Why, *that's not even in Rome.*'

'We have a choice? We'll go see it.' American intonation was beginning to overwhelm me.

'But it's a *village.* I mean, squalor, know what I mean?'

'It's squalid enough living in one room in a *pensione.*'

'*Centro storico,*' C observed, reading through the advertisement again, looking on the bright side. 'We'll have a look.'

And so we did, driving out north along the Via Cassia into the Roman Campagna, into Etruria, into an exhausted volcanic landscape still pockmarked by craters. Now the volcanoes are dead and the land is dissected by streams and cut into surprising gorges. Now oak forests grow at the base of the cliffs and sheep graze on the uplands and the hillsides are planted with olive and vine; but still the place is redolent of its volcanic past. At one point the smell of rotten eggs from some volcanic vent filled the car.

'Not me,' Natale assured us, adding optimistically, 'Good for the sinuses.'

The road wound down into a valley, then climbed and ran on across a grassy downland. There were shepherds' huts on the pastures and tumuli which marked the graves of Etruscan nobles. We saw the occasional, the very occasional, modern house of unmitigated awfulness. And then, round a bend in the road, there was the village.

Our road had come, it transpired, onto one side of a deep valley. To the right a track led down through *macchia* to the valley floor. The far wall of the valley was brown cliff, the rough brown volcanic tuff that has the appearance and almost the texture of dry fruitcake. In the middle of this valley, on a spur of the same rock, rose the village of Avea.

It was difficult to see where rock ended and building began. The one blended into the other in a manner which was purely instinctive, purely native, the natural artistry of people who

12

would have laughed at the idea of being so called. But who or when these people were was not clear. The place might have been a hundred, might have been a thousand, years old. It was stained and battered like a tramp steamer, pointing down the valley towards us with a prow that was blunted by age and weather. Trees rose up at the foot like a bow wave. The slab sides were pierced with windows just as though they had been portholes. The campanile was like a funnel rising up above the stepped, terracotta roofs. And just as though it were a ship seen on the high seas I felt that we were glimpsing Avea in the midst of some great voyage, through time perhaps.

At our insistence Natale stopped the car and we climbed out to look.

'What'd I tell you? Squalid!'

I looked at the place in delight. C viewed it with a more circumspect, Mediterranean eye: 'We'll see.'

We climbed back into the car and continued through a straggling modern suburb, then round the head of the valley and up towards the crenellated walls of an ancient *palazzo*. The main gate was a dark cave. Outside, in what passed for the twentieth century, there was a small piazza and a bar with tables set out beneath the trees. As we parked and climbed out of the car old men watched us from behind barricades of cloudy white wine. Clearly we were *forestieri*. The word means stranger, but the etymology is obvious: those from the forests, the tinkers and the charcoal-burners. Queer folk.

Natale went over for instructions and there was a long exchange and a waving of hands, mainly but not entirely towards the dark maw of the village gateway. Smiling thanks, we plunged through the opening and into the *centro storico*.

For some reason *centro storico* is always translated as 'historic centre', but that doesn't work in English. Forget the 'historic' nonsense. It sounds like something got up by the National Trust. We plunged through the gate from an approximate – very approximate – simulacrum of the twentieth

13

century into a leftover from the thirteenth. Not a deliberate preservation; just something someone seemed to have forgotten. Even the village gate, warped and riddled with woodworm, hung there on its iron hinges.

'They probably still shut it at sundown,' Natale muttered.

Beyond the gate the tiny piazza was as dark and dank as a well, floored with basalt setts – *selci* – and walled with grey volcanic rock. Steps on the left led up to the door of the *palazzo* but the door itself was barricaded and a notice announced that it had been closed for reasons of safety. Alongside the *palazzo* – palace is just not the word – was the village church. The far side of the square was occupied by the Municipio, the council offices, and in the furthest corner was an opening into an alley. It was, of course, Via Vittorio Emanuele II, the *strada principale*. A gutter ran down the centre. The stones of both walls were scoured at hip height where cars had scraped past.

'See what I mean?' said Natale, gesturing down this runnel. 'The only new thing is the name of the street, and that's a century out of date.'

On the corner of the alley was the only sign of life in the whole place, a flower shop from which vivid blossoms spilled out on to the basalt. As we passed, a voice came out of the shadows, broad and rasping in its Neapolitan tones and as foreign to this strange, involuted place as a drunk singing in a monastery.

'*Che cazzo fa' qui?*' It asked. C winced. The owner of the voice emerged and regarded us with a mixture of amusement and disbelief. She was a small, pugnacious woman, perhaps little older than C but certainly a great deal more aged. She had the arms and build of a bantam-weight boxer, and a face which blended raw humour with a curious simplicity of expression. Half-hidden behind her heavily lidded eyes was a profound tiredness. She exchanged a few words with Natale, rasping her voice up and down the scale like a combination of apprentice carpenter and inexpert violinist, shouting with laughter at something he said. When he introduced us – *gli stranieri* – she wiped her right hand on her apron before deciding that, even then, it was too dirty to shake. As a compromise she held out the little finger for each of us to take.

'*Piacere. Piacere.*' The compliments were perfunctory. '*Grazia.*'

I wondered what we had done to deserve thanks.

'Her name,' C explained. 'Grazia is her name.'

So I mumbled my own, knowing that my foreign intonation would render it unintelligible. But C's she understood immediately.

'*Sei siciliana allora?*'

'*Maltese.*'

'*Maltese?*' Wonders would never cease. She laughed hoarsely. '*È che cazzo fa' qui?*' she repeated.

And so it was explained to the flower lady what the bugger we were doing there. Did she know where the Piazza San Giuseppe was? Did she perhaps know of any places for rent? She answered the first question readily enough. In response to the second she tipped her head back and tutted her tongue against her teeth in the negative which I knew so well from C's island. It is a raw, negative, Arab gesture which has spread north up the Italian peninsula as far as Naples.

'*Allora, niente da fare,*' Natale replied. Nothing doing, then. He added, for politeness, '*Un bel paese, però.*' It's a beautiful village.

And Grazia roared with laughter. '*Bello? Ma vaffanculo!*' Even to one whose Italian was as inexpert as mine, that clearly amounted to marked disagreement.

'She's a bit rough,' Natale muttered as we crept away. It seemed a masterly understatement. Still laughing at the absurdity of foreigners Grazia, the Neapolitan *fioraia*, watched us dive into the alley to find our house.

Down one of the alleys leading off from the Via Vittorio Emanuele, amongst a jumble of similar cottages, was the place we were seeking. It was simply impossible to understand where one house left off and another began. The buildings were piled one against the other, like children's bricks abandoned in the middle of a game, the foundations of one forming the attic of another. But we found a tiny *piazzetta* blessed with the name of San Giuseppe and there, beside one door, was the number 5. In the wall nearby was a little shrine to the Madonna, with fresh flowers in a beer bottle before the statuette.

The key to the house was held by the neighbour, an ancient and red-nosed *contadino* whom we found outside his own cottage working on his most prized possession – an ancient Motoguzzi motorbike. With great solemnity he led us up the three steps to the tiny cottage that constituted *BICAMERA CON SERVIZI, CUCINA* and flung open the door. Damp wafted out at us. We peered in at little more than a cave.

'Okay?' said Natale, turning to go. 'Let's be heading back, then.'

I stopped him. C had vanished inside. I looked round, at the steep ramp which led back up to the main street, at the red roofs and grey walls, at the ancient chaos of the place. The village seemed to envelop us like some indifferent but benign organism. Over the years it had spawned, nurtured and digested thousands of inhabitants, hundreds of thousands no doubt. We were nothing. We could come or go as we wished. It was a curious moment, almost like one of Joyce's epiphanies. An instant of caprice would mean that we would live here amidst almost mediaeval confusion. A moment of common sense would put us back to hunting for an apartment amongst the dull suburbs of the city. In that moment I felt the essence of choice. Pure caprice.

'What are you up to?' I called, following her in.

From the living room there were five steps up into the bedroom with its corner shower cabinet and lavatory; and a turn of stairs led down into the kitchen. This truly was a cave, the real thing with rock walls and chisel marks and a kind of fungus growing on God knows what organic

16

matter above the ancient gas cooker. *BICAMERA CON SERVIZI, CUCINA*. Optimistic in the extreme. The house had two rooms and a cave, on three different floors, the biggest space no more than four metres by four. I collided with C on the stairs from the kitchen and she grinned at me.

'Calypso's cave.'

'What do you think?'

'Think? It's idiotic. But it's somewhere. And once we are here we'll find somewhere better. You'll see.'

'But that awful woman said there was nothing.'

C laughed. 'There isn't anything for casual strangers. But this is a village' – she qualified it – 'a *Mediterranean* village. Once we're living here, you'll see . . .'

Outside, Natale was discussing the finer points of pre-war Motoguzzi bikes with the old man. It seemed there was a carburettor part that you couldn't find . . .

'Finished?' Natale said, looking up.

'I think we've only just begun,' C replied.

# 2

The landlord lived in Rome, in the Monte Parioli district. He was charming, and slightly stooped from a lifetime, one imagined, of bowing over ladies' hands. I watched how he brought his lips like a precision instrument to within a millimetre of C's fingers without actually touching flesh.

'*Molto lieto di conoscervi.*' He was delighted to meet us. He was, amongst other things, a *commendatore*. He was also a Fascist. I use the term technically rather than as a form of abuse: on the piano in his sitting room was a framed photograph of a fresh-faced proto-*commendatore* wearing blackshirt uniform and shaking hands with Il Duce. For some reason Mussolini was wearing jodhpurs and a shirt which looked like a trophy from a cossack jumble sale, but never mind: the huge jaw and domed head were familiar enough without the trappings of Fascist regalia.

The *commendatore* saw my glance. 'Ah, I was younger then,' he said, wistfully stating the obvious. 'They were stirring times . . . but sad ones. We had such hopes, and they were dashed. Of course England was not our true enemy, you understand. We admired England, just as your Mr Churchill admired Il Duce. It was the Bolsheviks we did not want, nor the Americans. If we had not been caught in the war . . .'

It is in the nature of that Italian Fascism which still survives to give the impression that things went sadly wrong through no fault of their own. It is a creed much given to rose-tinted, or, if that metaphor is inappropriate, black-edged, reminiscence. Across a hillside high in the Apennine mountains, on the Via Salaria in fact, the message DVX is still emblazoned

18

for all the world to admire, written on the hillside in almost indelible letters many metres high – a carefully shaped plantation of trees. Political topiary. There is something emblematic about the whole thing, as there was something emblematic about the *commendatore*'s photograph of himself in his stirring youth shaking hands with Benito Mussolini. By the time the memento can be appreciated in all its glory – the trees have grown to maturity, the man is in his gentle retirement – the whole thing has become something of an embarrassment. Those who still really believe in the whole Fascist claptrap have to do an awful lot of shouting to keep their spirits up. Unfortunately they also occasionally blow innocent people to smithereens in the process.

'And the *signora* is from Malta?' the *commendatore* asked, releasing C's hand with apparent reluctance. '*Una isola affascinante.*' For a moment I thought he said 'Fascist', but he meant fascinating, charming. '*Italia irredenta,*' he added, with an ironic smile, voicing Mussolini's claim that Malta was unredeemed Italy, historically part of the peninsula. As with much of Il Duce's history, a schoolboy could have put him right.

'And now it is that you come and live in Italy? I hope that our tiny house in Avea is comfort enough for you. It has great character but' – he spread his hands helplessly – 'little *space.*'

'It is lovely,' C said nobly. 'I'm sure we will be happy. And the village is very beautiful. Maybe we will find something a little bigger later on.'

'*Certamente. Dopo ci siano altri in famiglia?*' He made an expansive gesture with the hand in front of his belly.

Not another one, I thought. In those early days my knowledge of Italian was patchy. Understanding jumped from one familiar word to another with little but guesswork to help me with what went on in between. It was like watching a scene by the light of a stroboscope: what happened in the darkness was the essential part, the part that made sense of the fixed and frozen images – but that was the part denied me. Now I had a hideous vision of the *commendatore* snatching our cave

19

in Avea away from us on the fictitious grounds of C's pregnancy. And she was slim. Slim! Like Calypso herself, I imagined. And this time she wasn't even wearing that bloody tent-like dress which had done for us on the Via Salaria.

'No, she's not,' I said loudly. Desperately I added, *'Non è pregnante.'*

Natale and C spluttered with laughter. The *commendatore* smiled sympathetically. Not everyone's idea of a Fascist. *'Incinta,'* he corrected me. 'I say soon she will be, no? Not yet but soon, right? Then you find a palace! Then the little house is not enough grand.'

I felt a pathetic wave of relief, and then laughter at his own words. That of course was our problem, the reason for renting a hole in the ground in the first place – we didn't have enough grand. But how on earth was I going to put that into Italian?

We moved in immediately, dumped with the two suitcases outside the main gate of the village because the van which brought us was too wide to enter. The same old men stared at us, apparently from behind the same jugs of cloudy white wine. Their expressions were suspicious. Doubtless their own ambitions were to leave their hovels in the old village for concrete and breeze-block monsters in the suburbs of Avea, for it is never the rustic peasant who appreciates failing water and uncertain electricity and roofs which leak. But there is no accounting for the habits of *forestieri*. Lugging our cases like refugees we walked past the tables, smiling and *buon giorno*ing all the way. They nodded and smiled in reply but still we gained the shadows of the village gate with a sensation of relief.

As we crossed the piazza a cry of greeting came from the depths of the apparently clientless flower shop – *'Salve!'* In this curious and involuted place the flower woman seemed almost emblematic of civilisation. At least she too was a foreigner, an intruder within the walls, a city person marooned in the *campagna*.

'*Salve!*' we called back.

Down the slope from the alley, Piazza San Giuseppe seemed even smaller than before. The moribund Motoguzzi still lay there like the victim of a road accident, bits of its carburettor strewn on the ground. Beyond it the house, *numero civico cinque*, seemed even more like a dwelling for troglodytes.

'Did we really mean this?' C asked uncertainly as she fiddled with the keys. But the little statue of the Madonna in its shrine seemed benevolent enough. The two suitcases almost filled the living room. Yet when we turned on the taps in the kitchen, against all odds the water ran; when we flipped a switch, the lights came on; when we bounced on the bed, the mattress sprang back resolutely.

'It's not so bad,' I reassured her. 'At least it's an improvement on that bloody *pensione* – the bed doesn't creak. What was it the old Fascist said? Additions to the family, was that it?'

So we celebrated our arrival by doing what had surely been done in the *centro storico* of Avea since time out of mind.

Avea and places like it need some explanation. Indeed the whole of the region in which Rome stands, ancient Latium, modern Lazio, needs an explanation. Latium is of course the land of the Latins, the people which gave Rome her language – but the Latins came from the south. The people to the north of the city – immediately to the north, breathing down Romulus' and Remus' necks, so to speak – were the Etruscans. When Rome was still a collection of shepherds' huts, the Etruscans had their own language and a great and elegant culture to go with it. They were rich, they were refined, they were powerful. They were, probably, the future.

Of course, no budding power like upstart Rome could tolerate such neighbours a mere dozen miles from its territory and soon enough the new city came into conflict with them; soon enough the first legions were on the move across the border just a few miles to the south of Avea. One imagines a grim, revolutionary mob bursting into a palace and laying about it

in a mixture of self-righteousness and envy. They stole the statues and the paintings, they stole the gods, they stole the trappings and the trivia, but they did not, could not, steal the culture.

The whole process of conquest took centuries. It was the usual mixture of war and appeasement and temporary peace and betrayal and massacre. There was destruction by fire and the sword, there was destruction by the insidious weapon of settlement, and by the time it was over that border between Latium and Etruria had been shifted a hundred miles north. All this happened well over two thousand years ago but its effects are still there, preserved like flies in the amber of the place names. The Etruscans were known to themselves as Rasenna, but no one remembers that except the owners of the bar beside the main gate of Avea. To the Greeks they were Tyrrhenoi, which gives us the Tyrrhenian Sea; to the Romans they were Etrusci or Tusci. That name has become, of course, Tuscany.

22

'*Gli Etruschi*? *Sono tutti morti*!' Thus one of Avea's worthies, laughing from behind his glass of cloudy wine. But, whether they are alive in spirit or dead as the histories and the villager tell us, the very name of the village, in its old form Aveia, harks back to them. Avea lay within the territory of the nearest Etruscan city to Rome, the first enemy city to be destroyed by the legions, the place from which the magnificent terracotta Apollo came. It was called Veii.

Autumn is the loveliest season in Italy and in those early weeks C and I walked a great deal in the countryside around the village. We watched the woods change from green to flame; we felt the air – as hot and opaque as wool in August – veer towards the north and bring clarity and the first thrilling hint of winter down from the mountains. During the day the light dazzled; as the afternoon wore on, it slanted low and turned to peach and rose. In the chill of the evenings acrid wood-smoke drifted over the rooftops of the village, the scent etching itself into the mind so deeply that now, wherever, whenever, I smell woodsmoke I am back in central Italy at the year's end.

We found streams and waterfalls and secret gorges, and traces of old Etruria left in the fabric of the land as clearly as a potter's thumb-print in a pot: carved tombs which the *contadini* now used for storing farm implements, tunnels and steps cut in the rock, fragments of pottery buried in the soil. We walked over the hill from the village and came upon a hidden valley and the sanctuary of the Madonna del Melagrano, the Madonna of the Pomegranate Tree; we found the ruins of La Mola, the water mill, with its huge grindstones still lying in the grass by the stream bank; we explored the site of Veii and the hot springs; we found our minds awakening to a complex of civilisation which is older than Christianity, as old as time – historic time – itself. The word *pagano*, pagan, is just the Latin word for a countryman or a villager – *paganus*. And wherever we wandered what struck us most was the very absence of the conqueror, the very absence of Rome, either ancient or modern.

'*I Romani*?' The same man – we dubbed him the Cowman – from behind the same jug of wine, but now his voice is tinged with contempt, because he has misunderstood and is talking not of the ancient Romans but the modern ones. 'They're just pigs, ill-educated pigs.' SPQR: *Senatus Populus-Que Romanus*. But also *Sono Porchi, Questi Romani*: They're Pigs, These Romans. Which makes attitudes clear enough but doesn't explain the wildness of the countryside, the empty wooded hills, the pastures unsullied by building, the olive groves, the vineyards all left to the casual wanderer almost as though the twentieth century had not happened. Ancient or modern, where were the Romans?

'*A Roma*,' the Cowman explained patiently. 'But wait till Sunday.'

And on Sunday they did come, a few of them anyway, nosing round the roads in their Sunday cars on the lookout for a trattoria. Only briefly would they halt the car in the Piazza Garibaldi in front of the village gate and gaze in wonder at the ancient grey walls and the rotting crenellations. '*Carina*,' they would say vaguely. Cute. And then they would shrug and pile back into the car like a detachment of an invading army that has found nothing worth plundering.

Rome was, of course, the first modern metropolis on earth. At its height, in Imperial times, it was a city of one million inhabitants from every part of the Empire, but by then the Etruscans had been destroyed or absorbed. Their language survived for a while but only in the remotest villages. Perhaps they spoke Etruscan into Imperial times in the village of Avea. Anyway, the external threat to the city of Rome had long been pushed far away, to the *limes* along the Rhine and the Danube, or to the deserts of Parthia and the mountains of Persia. The Etruscans were no longer a problem and once the threat had gone it became perfectly respectable, even fashionable, to claim Etruscan blood. The first wife of the emperor Claudius was Etruscan and her husband even wrote a history of the Etruscan people. In those later days being Etruscan must have been a bit like being Welsh or Scottish today.

But, for all its immense power, an internal danger did remain to Rome – the fundamental danger of starvation. Bread and Ciruses are a fine way to keep a people quiet, but you need to produce the bread. So the Campagna soon took on the role of bread basket and Veii and other cities were ploughed over and planted with wheat. Propertius, in the first century BC, struck the mood:

> Veii, thou hadst a royal crown of old,
> And in thy forum stood a throne of gold;
> Thy walls now echo but the shepherd's horn,
> And o'er thine ashes waves the summer corn.

But costs rose, as costs will, and for its grain the metropolis turned to Sicily and, when Sicily was exhausted, to Egypt. The fate of Southern Etruria was obvious: the people were dispossessed to make way for slaves and cattle. It sounds familiar – a classical version of the Highland Clearances, per-haps: the kind of upheaval which transforms a landscape. Priced out of the market and stripped of its inhabitants, the ancient land of the Etruscans plunged into decline. When the Empire finally collapsed, as empires will, Etruria was ruined almost beyond repair. Malaria and poverty and the rule of the Church and the feudal barons took over. Malaria is of course *mal aria*, bad air, and when he wandered this countryside in the middle of the last century George Dennis still found it rife. One town was 'but the skeleton, though a still living skeleton, of its former greatness. Pestilence, year after year, stalks through its long silent street.'

Malaria, poverty, the dead hand of the Church and the murderous hand of feudal barons. The land north of Rome was Orsini country. Their arms still stand over the gate of Avea for the Roman visitor to squint at with little understanding before he climbs back into the car and drives on to the trattoria for Sunday lunch. The Orsini were one of the two great families of mediaeval and renaissance Rome – the other is the Colonna. Between them they disputed the city and the Papacy from the Dark Ages to the Renaissance and beyond – the last Orsini Pope was Benedict XIII in 1724. Such families did well enough for themselves, but they didn't do much for the peasants who lived in their fiefs. Depressed and deserted during the Roman Empire, exploited and crushed by their rulers ever since, ridden with malaria until the early years of this century, it was only with the land reforms after the Second World War that most of the *contadini* came into possession of the land which they had worked more or less as slaves since the Romans first occupied Etruria. That is another lesson I learned quickly when talking to the Cowman at his table in the Piazza Garibaldi.

'*Eravamo schiavi!*' he insisted, sounding each syllable with elaborate emphasis lest the point be lost in his country accent. We were slaves! His audience grinned and jeered, but he told the truth. For the people of Avea the good old days simply weren't.

Early autumn is the time of the *vendemmia*. Families were out in the vineyards and tubs of grapes were on the move round about the village, occasionally on the backs of donkeys but more often pulled on trailers behind tiny, chuttering tractors. The sharp scent of crushed grape hung in the alleyways. Piles of grape pressings, brown and acetic, appeared outside the cellars and we peered down into ancient caves where the vats seethed and the barrels stood like totems. Fruit flies, *moscioni*, hung hopefully in the air and met inebriated deaths in one's wine glass.

'*Un buon' segno,*' a good sign, Oreste assured us, lifting a carafe of his own wine – as brown as mahogany – to the light to display a small mortuary of the animals at the bottom. He was the garlic man, the nut man, his face as brown as his wine, his legs hideously bowed. Grinning at us with gappy brown teeth, he filled up our glasses yet again. '*Vino genuino*,' he insisted. 'No chemicals.'

I regret that in this organic, macrobiotic age Oreste's assertions sound more laudable than they are. What his wine needed was precisely what he withheld – chemicals. Sour as soon as fermented, it was desperate for sulphur dioxide: sulphur dioxide to clean the casks, to stun the spoilage yeasts and bacteria, to arrest the oxidation which turned the colour to mahogany. But you couldn't say that and if you did you wouldn't be believed, so you drank it and kept smiling. And indeed, with Oreste and his wife, there was a good deal to smile about. They lived in a hovel in the valley immediately outside the old village, one room down, one room up, a lavatory added outside as an afterthought. The family name was Buonarotti, which was good for a grin, and life, surely the cruellest thing imaginable, seemed a huge joke. He would hammer his awful, twisted knees and laugh. 'Useless!' he would exclaim. 'Ruined.' Ruined, in fact, by the Russian winter of 1942/1943.

It was difficult to imagine Oreste anywhere but in Avea, selling nuts and dried fruit at his stall just outside the main gate or inviting you into his house to inspect strings of plump garlic bulbs which hung maturing in the shadows. It was difficult to imagine him even in Rome, the metropolis which the maps insisted was just on the horizon but which common sense told you was a universe away in every quality other than distance. But it was impossible to imagine him in Russia.

He shrugged, with the ineffable fatalism of the Italian *contadino*. 'We went by train. Rome, Bologna, Brennero. I don't know – Austria, Germany, Poland, Russia. Russia, Russia, Russia.' It was all one to him, the great steppe where the open sky pressed down with indifferent weight on serf and *contadino* alike. Light years away from the intimate countryside of Avea with its hills and valleys, its sudden gorges, its woodlands and vineyards and orchards. Oreste laughed at the memory. 'Nowhere to hide. Nowhere to run.' And in the shadows of his living room, with his wife looking on fondly – 'Drink, drink!' – his gnarled hands would take over the job of words, circling over the table and diving towards the wine glasses. 'Eeeeeooooowww! Dadadadada! Eeeeeeeeeoooowww!' Like a schoolboy at play, except that he had seen the planes with the red stars on their fuselages, and the tracer bullets streaking from their wings. Two thousand miles from home he had felt the terror.

'They came at us over the ice. Tanks, tanks on the ice over the river.' He laughed at the absurdity of it. 'There was nowhere to hide. Nowhere to go. And the snow! The cold!'

Along with thousands of Italians, Oreste had walked from the banks of the Don, walked and walked and walked across the winter steppe with nowhere to go except away. And, gesturing with his hands above his head, he laughed at the memory. 'Snow, snow this high! Forty degrees below zero!'

Finally he was captured by the Red Army. 'To Siberia.' The names had gone now, if he had ever known them then. 'Siberia, Siberia.' His gesture encompassed greater spaces than the mind could comprehend.

'He came back to me in 1951,' his wife said with a smile.

Ten years, nine of them in Soviet prison camps in Siberia. Difficult to imagine Oreste outside Avea. But easy to imagine him getting down from the train at Termini Station, broken and ruined, and smiling at a country that had almost forgotten.

# 3

Flapping in the Piazza San Giuseppe, establishing our territory like mediaeval flags, our own washing joined the other
lines of shirts and underwear. Villagers nodded and smiled
as we passed by, anticipating rather than awaiting our own
greeting. We were, it seemed, *cristiani*. I was at work during
the day and so it was mainly C, flung rudely back into a way
of life that was fast disappearing in her own island, who made
the first contacts, first sensed the occult undercurrents of village life, the complex interrelationships, the jealousies, the
friendships, the estrangements.

'She's married to the butcher' – pointing to some anonymous
woman in black – 'and she's second cousin to Giuseppina –'

'Giuseppina?'

'You know, the *alimentari* woman. Now, through her husband she's also related to the man who runs the bar. And his
daughter is her son's *fidanzata*. You know, the young one with
the squint. Then there's the counter clerk in the bank. He's
some kind of relation as well, but they don't speak because . . .'

*Cugino, nuora, suocero, compare, zio, nonno, bisnonno,
prozia*, but only one word, *nipote*, to cover both grandchild
and nephew/niece. It is a complex, private world which is
discovered only piece by piece and then only by the patient.
The *paese* – the word is emblematic of an Italian attitude to
life: it means 'place' or 'village' or 'country', anywhere that
may signify home – the *paese* is not just the stones, not just
the people, but a complex interweaving of the two, warp and
weft combining to create that whole fabric which the passer-by
merely glances at and sees as a picturesque old village. Just to

shop there regularly was to begin to explore and unpick these strands: the butcher who was married to the woman in black and who seemed to found his entire trade on three pork chops and two sheeps' heads; the baker whose daughter was a problem and kept going off to Rome with dubious young men; and the endearing, motherly Giuseppina who ran the grocery shop and was the baker's *cugina*, but, more importantly, was Oreste's daughter.

'Her husband is the cousin of the bank manager, but he's useless.'

'The bank manager?'

'His brother, Giuseppina's husband. You're not concentrating. He's the black sheep of the family. Well, lame dog maybe. The family are all accountants or clerks or whatever but Giuseppina can't even get him to do the tax returns for the shop.'

'Tax returns? I thought that was a concept unknown to the Italians.'

'They have to do something, even if it's lies.'

'I imagine it's even more difficult if it is lies.'

On Sundays Giuseppina sold *porchetta* from a stall in the main square outside the gate. This was like something from a mediaeval feast, a whole pig from snout to tail roasted over a wood fire. We went to watch the immolation in the yard behind Oreste's house one Saturday. The family had gathered for the event. The walls of the village rose like a grey cliff over the scene. As Giuseppina skewered the pig with a wooden stake the audience's comments were clear in meaning but uncertain in detail. The word *culo* featured prominently. The wretched beast had already been stuffed with a pounded mixture of fennel, rosemary, garlic and nutmeg. Once impaled, it was manipulated by Oreste into the oven. There was much grunting and laughter but for all the amusement there was something sacrificial about the whole affair, as though we were offering the beast up to Jupiter or Bacchus or some other ancient deity of the place.

'It's just as big as you!' they called out to Oreste.

'You look as if you're dancing!'

'It's warmer than Russia, I bet!'

'That's how you'll go,' Giuseppina shouted. 'Roasted in the flames!' They roared with laughter.

Once the pig was in place on the spit Giuseppina began pushing trunks of pine and holm oak into the blaze. She was a big woman, twice the size of her father, and with a great maternal dignity about her. 'Fresh wood,' she explained to us in case we were thinking of cooking entire pigs in our underground kitchen. 'You must use fresh wood during the cooking. It gives the flavour.' The oven seethed. She rolled her sleeves back and took up a long-handled basting spoon as though preparing to sup with the devil. At least her father's rough wine had some use. 'Baste often and cook it until it's golden. Maybe three hours.'

The next day, laid out cold and richly aromatic on a bier in the main piazza, the animal was sacrificed to the greed of a Sunday crowd. Close at hand was Oreste's own stall of dried nuts and fruit. The Buonarotti family, artists in their own way, were masters of the Sunday *passegiata*.

Amongst the growing number of people with whom we were on familiar terms there was, of course, our very first acquaintance, the woman who ran the flower shop next to the Municipio. One afternoon when I had just returned from work C informed me that I had been summoned.

'Her husband. We've got to go and meet her husband.'

'Why? I'm tired and I've got things to do. What do I want with a flower lady's husband?'

'She said that she might be able to help us with accommodation. We've got talking to each other. I told you how villages work. Now you have to meet the husband.'

And so we shut the house and walked to the little square inside the main gate. Flowers spilled out from the shop as though from a cornucopia, bringing a splash of garish colour to the sombre piazza.

'*Salve*!' cried Grazia. Amongst the stolid natives she was unmistakably a creature from the south, from the place where people made a noise, lived their lives in public, shouted and wept and laughed across streets. '*Entrate*! *Entrate*!'

We passed into the narrow shadows of her shop between tubs of lilies and roses and peonies. The air was heavily perfumed.

'*Gli stranieri*,' she announced to a figure seated in the darkness. '*Ecco Pippo*!'

Do I imagine it now or did her rough, Neapolitan voice have an edge of mockery to it as she announced her husband's presence? She gestured towards the dark figure and in retrospect it was like going to see some exhibit, the fat woman perhaps or the man with two heads, in a country fair. There, ensconced in shadow, enthroned amongst flowers, he waited.

Pippo was a grotesque. One has to consider him in parts and carefully, and then hold all those parts in your mind at once to get the whole. It is an unnerving undertaking. He

32

appeared to be composed of elements that were constantly at war with one another, features and contours which struggled incessantly for dominance over the battleground of his body. He was diminutive, but vast; his black hair hung in ringlets to his shoulders, but on top he was running to baldness; his face was as huge as a pumpkin, but his feet were tiny almost to invisibility; his expansive upper lip was decorated with a moustache of razor thinness and precision, but his manifold chins were rough with stubble; his expression was cunning but his eyes were those of a simpleton. Somehow he gave the appearance of being at the same time both the organ grinder and the monkey.

'*Piacere*,' he rumbled. The hand which he thrust out to shake ours was beringed with gold and blackened with grime. The nail of his little finger was carefully cultivated to a length that would have done a Balinese dancer proud; needless to say, no other feature of his body seemed even to be made of the same substance as a Balinese dancer.

As he eyed C his lips curled wolfishly. '*Che bella signora.*'

I noticed that his glance kept going to a mirror which hung on the wall, just to make sure, I presumed, that he really did look as magnificent as he thought. For Pippo was nothing if not self-deluding. He imagined that he was rich, he imagined he was *un bel uomo*, he imagined that he was cunning and clever – the word, and a very important concept it is too, is *furbo* – he imagined that he was powerful. He was none of these, but the important thing is the belief. He probably also believed that he was virtuous, although that is one quality he never boasted of to me. On the other hand he did so on behalf of his first wife and, as it is the Italian female who usually acts as a kind of surrogate for her husband in the matter of religious observance, I suppose it amounts to the same thing: ''*na santa*,' he would say of her. A saint. And tears, real tears, would start to his eyes. One could not deny their reality, nor the reality of the emotion which underlay them. Contrary to the popular image which holds sway in Anglo-Saxon countries, the Italians are a hard-headed nation, a nation of doers, of workers, of earners and savers. There is nothing profligate about them – except when it comes to emotion. They spend emotion readily enough because it is free.

'She was a saint. She died in my arms, my arms' – holding them out in case I had missed them – 'and she said, "Who will look after you when I am gone, Filippo? Who will keep you from harm?"'

Who indeed? 'There is Grazia,' I reminded him. This was later, when we had been invited home for lunch. At my words he glanced resignedly at his second wife standing over the pasta, enveloped in steam. 'Grazia,' he repeated without conviction. Grazia, you see, was not a saint. She was all too humanly Neapolitan. He could betray Grazia without compunction; but to betray his first wife required real commitment. '*'Na santa, nel nome di Dio 'na vera santa.*' Not poor Grazia.

Out of that first encounter and the invitation to lunch came our new flat.

'You can't go on living in that hole in the ground,' Grazia said with a disparaging tilt to her chin. 'It's not fit. You need somewhere modern, a bit of room.'

'Room for babies,' added Pippo. 'Like this place.' He waved his arms proudly. Their own flat, outside the *centro storico* of course, occupied the top floor of a small *palazzo* which Pippo owned. 'A place with a bit of room. Room for babies,' he said, grinning lasciviously at C across mountainous plates of spaghetti. Red sauce glistened on his chin. 'How long have you been married?' he asked.

'Three years,' said C.

He tutted and shook his head. Spaghetti disappeared into the great maw. 'You know what we say? Eh? You know? If a tree doesn't give fruit' – he raised his chin and drew a grimy thumb across his neck – 'cut it down!'

Grazia looked at him reproachfully from her place at the log fire in the corner of the kitchen. They had been married

34

for eight years now and there were no children. In Pippo's eyes Grazia was a barren tree; but then he had no children by the saint either. Perhaps, I reflected, the barrenness lay in the workings of Pippo's own body.

'Anyway,' said Grazia, 'you must come and live with us.'

Was she suggesting the spare room? 'With you?'

She roared with laughter and pointed towards the floor with a fork. '*Giù.* In our *palazzo*, in the flat downstairs. We've just had it fixed. You can move in there. Into our *palazzo*.'

It is all too easy to find cause for amusement in a foreign language when none really exists: the word *palazzo* needs some explanation. It is not hyperbole. The Italian *palazzo* is not only the English 'palace', a vast mansion for the exclusive occupation of princes or dukes or Snow Whites, although it may be that as well. The Italian palace is the direct heir of the renaissance town palace which tourists gawp at in Florence or Venice or Rome, the noble building which had artisans' workshops on the ground floor, the great family's apartments on the *piano nobile*, and above that, in a warren of further rooms and floors, the homes of lesser relatives and client families. This kind of palace is something organic, something which grows both in time and space, a place in which families of every class may live and a multitude of trades may be pursued. In spirit, if not in superficial appearance, it is a thing far removed from mere 'block of flats'. It was thus with the Palazzo Doria in Rome and the Palazzo Medici-Riccardi in Florence; and was thus with Pippo's *palazzo* in Avea: on the ground floor a diminutive grocery store and a motorcycle-repair shop, on the next floor the tenants, and above all – the only change from the traditional form – above all, the apartment of the *padrone*, an apartment which gleamed with pink marble and dark, varnished wood. There was a plaster model of the Madonna and a picture of the Sacred Heart of Jesus, as well as a large, soft-focus photograph of Pippo's first wife looking every bit the plaster saint. The kitchen where we ate would have housed a snooker table with ease. *Un palazzo.*

35

Grazia raked embers from the fire on to the brick apron in front, then heaved an iron grill into place before turning to ladle more pasta on to our plates. In vain we protested that we had eaten more than enough. 'You can move in when you like,' she said. 'Tomorrow. We were going to have a cousin there but it's too small for him now his wife's pregnant again.'

'*Incinta*,' Pippo repeated with glee.

'So . . .'

'But we've got a contract for the house in the *centro storico* . . .'

Grazia was back at the fire. Steaks, piles of steaks, seethed on her grill. 'Do you know it?' she asked Pippo. 'Do you know the place? The one that Roman bastard owns, next to Angelo. A hole, nothing but a hole in the ground.' She turned to face us. 'How much do you pay?' Conversation with Grazia was like being shot at by a sub-machine-gun in the hand of an expert. The bullets hit you suddenly and precisely in short sharp bursts. 'How much?'

'*Cento mila.*'

'*Cento mila!*' This was more like an anti-tank weapon firing shaped charges, driving holes through armour plate. '*Cento Mila? Sono ladroni quei bastardi!*'

'It seemed a bargain to us.'

'A bargain? It's just a hole in the rock. A tomb.'

I felt defensive about our little house. '*Caracteristico*,' I explained, stumbling over the syllables. '*Carino.*'

'Ah,' Grazia corrected me. '*CarinA*. And it's not.' Her hoarse voice shot the idea to pieces in a blast of rapid fire. I only grasped the word *porcile*.

'What's a *porcile*?'

'A pigsty,' C answered. I might have guessed. We lived in a pigsty.

Pippo belched volubly and wiped sauce from his chin with a napkin that looked like a swab from an operating theatre. Shaking his head in disbelief at the depths to which his fellow countrymen could sink, he offered his idea. 'I tell you what.

I'm an honest man. I tell you what I'll do. You can have the flat for the same amount. One hundred thousand lire. It's a gift.'

Grazia nodded. It was largesse from *un signore*, benevolence from a great *padrone*.

'We'll have to think about it,' C replied cautiously.

Pippo waved his arms. 'Think, think. But don't delay. Apartments here are like gold dust. They'll be hammering on my door.'

Grazia slid plates of grilled steak in front of us. On all the occasions we ate with them I never saw her sit at table for more than a minute at a time. Her place was preparing, and cooking, and clearing, and washing.

'*Magna, magna,*' Pippo demanded of us, gesturing with one hand as though shovelling food into his own capacious mouth. The word is Roman dialect – *maña*, like the first syllables of the Spanish *mañana*. It is a corrupted form of *mangia*, blended both in sound and meaning with *magno*, great. Snacks and fast food are strangers to the Roman *cucina*. '*Magna, magna. È bono*. Afterwards we'll have a look.'

We ate. Grazia piled more on our plates. We protested and ate further. More food, more protests, more eating. *Magna, magna*. Pippo belched once more and reached for a toothpick. Then he opened his mouth wide to display an array of teeth as brown as the keys of an ancient piano, and with elaborate care he began to mine them for interesting bits. The meal, it seemed, was finally at an end.


Afterwards we trooped down the stairs of the *palazzo* to examine the flat below. It was certainly bigger than the *porcile* – a bedroom at the back, a bathroom and kitchen in the middle, and a large living room at the front – but then it was also out of the *centro storico*, on the road leading to Rome.

'*Bello, bello,*' Pippo kept assuring us.

'But it hasn't yet been wired,' C pointed out. 'There's only lighting in the bedroom.'

'Just where you don't need it, eh?' Grazia spluttered with ribald laughter at her husband's joke. 'But don't worry, don't worry. I'll send the boy round immediately. Don't you worry about the wiring. It's yours for one hundred.'

'We'll think about it,' C repeated.

Pippo regarded us through narrowed eyes. 'You foreigners – *furbi*, eh?' Cunning. 'But admit it, it's a bargain. *Un bel apartamento.*'

We were not so confident. True to the best *palazzo* tradition the place was subject to constant adaptation and adjustment, but in this case the stimulus had been an order of closure by the Municipio on grounds of safety. The remains of the official seals could still be seen on the door jambs. I pointed to them.

'Subsidence,' Pippo said dismissively. 'Now everything's all right. Just the finishing touches to do.'

This was something of an understatement. Where it overlooked the main road the outside wall of the building was faced with naked cavity bricks of a fleshly pink. Ferroconcrete beams emerged from the flesh. Iron rods sprouted from them like bones poking out of a compound fracture. Multi-coloured wiring hung in elegant swags over the main entrance.

'A bit of plaster,' said Pippo.

In the very middle of this front wall, up on the first floor and suspended twenty feet above the ground, was a door.

I pointed. 'That's from the living room of the apartment. A door into open space.'

'A balcony,' Pippo assured us. He waved his arms boldly to encompass empty air and the ground-floor terrace where we stood. 'I'm going to build a balcony right out here.'

I looked up through his conceptual balcony. 'And meanwhile?'

C translated, '*Nel frattempo?*'

Pippo regarded us with shrewd eyes. We were definitely *furbi*. 'Meanwhile,' he repeated. 'Meanwhile you keep the door locked.'

# 4

'What do you think?'

'About what?'

'The new flat.' C was down the turn-of-stairs, in the kitchen. I was sitting on the lavatory in the shower box off the bedroom. We were two floors apart. We didn't have to shout.

'You sound as though you've already decided.'

'No, I haven't.'

'It's not in the *centro storico*.'

'It's not got damp either. And it has got room.' Our possessions lived in their two suitcases underneath the half-sized double bed. When you lay on the bed you could feel them there beneath you. It gave you a sensation of security.

'And a door open on to empty space,' I pointed out. 'And no wiring.'

'He said he'd install it.'

'He *said*.'

'I'll be here to see that he does. It'll give me something to do during the day.' I didn't doubt that. C had always worked until now and in Avea time was beginning to weigh heavily on her hands. And I had a suspicion she'd make a good match for Pippo. 'You can't really expect me to be happy living in this cave all day.'

'Perhaps there are other places. What about the Collasanti family?'

'*Colasanti*,' C corrected. The pronunciation of the single consonant is subtly different from the double. It's the kind of thing you point out when you're growing impatient. 'You know both their flats are occupied.'

'But maybe one of their tenants will move. Maybe she'll find something for us elsewhere.'

'Maybe I'll stay stuck in this cave for six months while we hope.'

We had met the Colasanti the first morning my *motorino* wouldn't start, which was almost the first morning I had tried to use it.

'It won't start,' I cried out to C in desperation. 'Christ, it won't start!'

'Blasphemy won't help.'

'How in God's name am I going to get to work?' I gave up my frantic pedalling, climbed off and glared helplessly at the machine, knowing nothing of its workings. The cylinder, a little box of flanged aluminium, looked no bigger than a packet of cigarettes and at that moment rather less incandes-

40

cent. Aroused by my wailing, our neighbour Angelo appeared at the door to his house. His ancient Motoguzzi still leaned inertly against the wall. He smiled warmly at me. Now we were not only neighbours but companions in adversity.

'*Cosa faccio?*' I asked helplessly, hoping for expert advice. He shrugged. '*Trova un passaggio.*' Find a lift.

'Thanks a lot.' I fiddled vainly with the engine and pedalled the machine desperately round the nearest alleys. Nothing pedals less convincingly than a dead *motorino*. Occasionally the packet of cigarettes sighed and spat at me. I stumbled back to the house exhausted.

'The expert's right,' I told C. 'You'll have to get me a lift.'

'*I'll* have to get you a lift?'

'A woman's touch. Come on, I know from experience. Italy's good for hitching even if you're a man; if you are a woman you command the place. Instant success. A bite every cast.'

I dragged her out to the Piazza Garibaldi and we waited for a likely vehicle. At the bar the *contadini* were drinking coffee with *grappa*, a brisk combination at eight in the morning. They watched stolidly as C failed to hook a three-wheeler truck as it buzzed past. It was one of those little things that career round the countryside with farm implements in the back, or tubs of grapes, or a pair of sheep. I could just imagine myself arriving at work in the back of that.

'I thought you said first try.'

'In a manner of speaking.'

C looked askance at me. Hitching was outside her experience. It smacked of begging.

'Go on, have another go.'

Fortunately salvation came soon. It appeared not from the road which passed through the square but from the bowels of the *centro storico* itself – and in the unlikely shape of a long white Maserati barely edging its way through the main gate. C waved enthusiastically and the incongruous car stopped beside us. The driver's window hummed down and Lorenzo

Colasanti smiled out with that bemused expression that the Italian reserves for the antics of foreigners. He was, we duly discovered, the owner of a large house at the end of the village.

'You are English perhaps?'

C pointed accusingly. '*He* is.'

'Perhaps you want *un passaggio*?'

'*Un passaggio* is exactly what I want.'

Lorenzo Colasanti: tall and grey and, C assured me, immensely attractive. So too, I could assure her, was his wife who sat beside him in the car. She possessed that particular elegance which is uniquely Italian. She wore exotic leather and the fur of many species. Gold glittered against the brown velvet of her skin as it might in a Gucci display case. Her legs were sheathed in black silk, her breasts were elevated against both age and gravity, and her face was a portrait of a renaissance courtesan painted by the school of Titian. She would have driven a conservationist mad, a puritan to distraction and a feminist to a mastectomy; but in Rome, even, absurdly, in Avea, she was magnificent. I wish to qualify that statement: *anywhere* she *ought* to have been magnificent – it is just that other countries are too feeble to come to terms with women like Pia. In London she would be suspected of being an oil sheikh's mistress. Her full name is, of course, Maria Pia – Holy Mary.

Beneath C's equivocal gaze I was invited to slide into the Maserati behind this magnificent creature. There was a miasma of expensive perfume.

'Where would you like to go?' she asked. In the mirror on the inside of her sun visor I saw dark eyes watching me.

'Wherever you are going.'

'Wherever?'

'I mean where. Where are you going? I don't want to take you out of your way.'

'It is no trouble.'

Lorenzo slipped the car into gear and we swept away from

the old village. Glancing over my shoulder I saw C watching suspiciously.

The Colasanti were, I suppose, the first Romans to discover Avea; on the other hand they had rights there because Lorenzo had been brought up in the village, the son of the local doctor. The same evening they invited us to their house. It lay at the end of the *centro storico*, at the very prow of the ship, round three sides of a little square with a single holm oak growing in the middle. One got the strong impression of a mediaeval family fortress barricaded against fortune. Inside, the floors glowed with the dark fire of terracotta. There were elegant archways in grey *peperino*, the hardest volcanic stone of the area, and a huge grey fireplace the size of a doorway. There were mighty chestnut beams to support the upper floors and an Etruscan tomb in the cellar. But the kitchen was a gleaming aluminium display of the latest kitchenware, like the cockpit of a jumbo jet.

'My husband inherited the house,' Pia explained. 'And we restored it. We had to do much work. And then we moved the factory nearby.'

They owned a plastics factory. That is another typical piece of Italy. To look at them you might have imagined the film industry or a fashion house; but what you got was a plastics factory making bathroom fitments. The catalogue lay negligently on a chair in their kitchen. It was like something published for a Henry Moore retrospective exhibition at the Tate Gallery, full of glossy full-page photographs displaying sinuous, organic objects posed beneath artfully angled spotlights. Only on minute inspection do they turn out to be lavatory-brush holders or soap dishes. The captions discussed 'plastic values' and 'tactile qualities' in four languages.

*Il Made in Italy* is the generic title for that kind of thing and there is a strange hint of irony about the phrase, as though the Italians themselves do not really take all this Italian design business seriously. It isn't dishonesty or cynicism, it is just

that the Italian is the great fatalist. All things come to an end;
the Roman Empire came to an end, Christ came to an end –
why should Italian economic success be any different? So
better not take it too seriously lest when the end does come it
breaks your heart.

Despite the splendour of her own house, Pia was very gra-
cious about our hole in the rock. '*Affascinante*,' she judged it.
'But rather small.' She reclined in a leather sofa with her legs
folded carefully beneath her so that one could see how perfect
they were. She was a magnificent negation of the old saw that
Italian women are beautiful when young but go to seed early.
Wherever Pia was, it was not at seed.

'We're looking for something rather bigger . . .'

A sigh. '*Ahimè*. If only we had something. We have only
just finished the three apartments next door, but already they
are occupied. We only let them to friends, of course. It makes
the whole building a kind of community.'

Of course we went round to consult her about Pippo's offer.

'Ah, *i Rozzi*.' Her tongue tripped lightly on the double
consonant. Her mouth wore a small, malign smile. Pippo's
surname was Rossi: *rozzo* means uncouth. There was a silence
amongst the antique furniture, the painted Florentine *cassone*,
the *intarsia* table. On the wall over her shoulder a nameless
goddess disported herself amongst a bevy of nymphs, each
one, I guessed, with a figure not dissimilar to Pia's own. Well,
make certain you read the small print,' she advised finally. 'Do
you say that in English? *Stampa piccola*.'

'Exactly.'

'You must come and give me conversation practice.'

'You don't need it. *I* need teaching Italian.'

She shrugged. 'It's an easy language. You will pick it up.
Although you must be a little careful of what you learn from
*i Rossi*.'

That, we guessed, signified approval of a kind.

44

The next morning, as I passed through the main gate and out into the twentieth century, I heard a shout.

'*O professor!*' Impossible to give the intonation, the swagger of it, the piercing tones of the Roman dialect. From his table beneath the trees Pippo flapped his hand at me to come across. '*Venga, venga.*'

I went over and was displayed to his cronies with the pride one might reserve for a new car – *er professor' inglese!* – and there was much nodding and smiling across the barrier of language. Names and ranks were exchanged. Pippo, it transpired, was *dottor*, doctor, which he plainly wasn't, either of medicine or philosophy. Italian titles are optimistic in the extreme, suffering from what one might term honorific inflation. The poorest graduate is granted a doctorate, and everyone else is given some kind of superior handle by degree or profession – *ingegnere, ragioniere, professore* – right up to the summit, where politicians reside like Olympian gods and revel in the appellation *onorevole*. At times it seems that the title bestowed describes exactly the opposite of the qualities possessed by the holder. Pippo's friends, with their gnarled hands and stubbled faces and battered, sweat-stained hats, were doctors every one. Hearing them you might have supposed yourself to be in a faculty room at Rome University rather than at a table in the Piazza Garibaldi in Avea, sitting underneath the holm oaks, drinking a thimble of pungent black coffee and playing *scopa*.

All this takes place within the confines of a language whose polite form is a curiously oblique and feminine third person – *Lei*. 'I am delighted to meet her,' they say to you, about yourself. 'Where does she come from?' they ask. By this strange form they are implicitly granting you yet another honorific, in this case the title of excellency. *Eccellenza* is of feminine gender – *Sua Eccellenza*. '*Come sta, Lei?*' someone may ask. 'How is she feeling?' She might be a navvy on a building site, bulging with muscle and devoid of brain, but nevertheless she is her excellency.

45

But there was more, and even more fantastically inappropriate. Pippo pointed up through the trees to the grey walls of the Palazzo which rose behind us. '*Professore*, that is where I used to live. Me and my brother, in that *palazzo*.'

I wanted to point out that it too had been closed as unsafe just like his present *palazzo*.

'I lived there with my first wife, God bless her soul. Ah, those days! You know what they called me then, eh? Me, my name?'

'*Venerabile?*' I hazarded.

'No.' But near. '*Er Duca. Er Duca di Avea.*' The Duke of Avea. He pounded his chest in emphasis, while his friends nodded and laughed. '*Duca*,' they called, pointing at him and clapping. '*Er Duca.*' I still don't know whether they were mocking him, but he had no doubt. He smiled benevolently on their display of loyalty. 'Oh, I had money then, lots of money. My wife and I were rich and happy. We would have had children . . .' His voice trailed away. 'You see that window?' I peered up where he pointed. A whole doctoral symposium peered with me. 'The one on the end with the balcony, you see it?'

We saw it.

'That is where she died . . . in my arms.' There was a catch in his voice. He was a tenor about to break into song, a Rodolfo about to mourn his Mimi, an Alfredo weeping over his Violetta. Tears welled in his eyes while the good ole boys nodded in sympathy. A grimy white handkerchief did its duty and the mood abruptly changed.

'And you, *professore*, and *la bella signora*' – his eyes were momentarily lascivious – 'have you decided? Are you going to take the apartment?' He turned to explain his largess to the audience and they looked satisfactorily impressed at the generosity being shown the Englishman. 'What have you decided?'

'Well, we haven't yet, not really. It's not in the *centro storico*, you see –'

46

'*Bello, lussuoso.*' That gesture again, as though cupping water from a basin, holy water from a stoop.

'And then there's the wiring in the kitchen –'

At once his voice boomed across the square. 'Romano!' A youth came across from the bar. Pippo gave him a quick blast of *romanesco* in which he assuredly did not use the *Lei*. The youth shrugged and held out helpless hands. There was another volley from Pippo and a resigned expression from Romano before he wandered away.

'*Ecco fatto,*' announced Pippo. All fixed. 'So you move in immediately.'

'But there's the problem of our stuff.' *Nostra roba* – a marvellous utility word one learns early. And *robaccia* is rubbish, which is perhaps how Pippo saw our few motley possessions.

'What stuff? A few suitcases. Grazia will carry them in her van.'

'And we'll have to contact the *commendatore*, to break the contract.'

'Grazia will deal with him, the robber. So it's decided?'

So it was decided. We got Natale to drive out to check over the new contract but it seemed to be all in order.

'A bit ripe, your new landlady,' he muttered once again. And the *commendatore*, summoned from Rome to take the house back, winced every time Grazia spoke. He was kind and understanding to us, even returning the three months' rent which we had put down as deposit. Perhaps he felt sympathy.

'Of course you need something more suitable,' he agreed. 'This is perhaps holiday home.' In an effort to be sympathetic I felt he was unnecessarily disparaging about number five Piazza San Giuseppe.

'It is a lovely little house,' I told him. 'Just a bit too little.'

'You are very kind.' Like a good Fascist he did not use the *Lei*, but rather the third person plural – *voi* – which is the southern form preferred by Mussolini. Il Duce had considered *Lei* archaic and actually tried to ban it, as though by mere decree one can change a language. It was yet another demonstration of the man's uncertain grip on reality.

We left some fresh flowers in the beer bottle at the foot of the Madonna and followed Grazia up to the Via Vittorio Emanuele to load our two suitcases into her Fiat van. The *commendatore* shook hands and wished us good luck: *'In bocc' al lupo.'* In the wolf's mouth. Perhaps he was referring to Grazia.

Thus, a month after our arrival, we left the *centro storico* of Avea for the suburbs, driving in state beside Grazia in her van with FIORISTA LA PRIMULA painted on the side. Pippo went before us as escort in his raging, red Alfa Romeo GTV, blasting our approach out on twin-tone wind horns. In the short journey – out of the main gate, past the bank and the primary school, round the head of the valley where there were the communal garden and war memorial, and back down via Roma past Giuseppina's supermarket and the filling station – we had two near misses.

As we climbed thankfully out of the van we looked up with mixed feelings at our new abode. The brickwork was still painfully exposed. Skeletal fingers of ferroconcrete still poked out of raw flesh. The french window still opened on to empty space. But at least it was all right inside. At least we'd have room to *girare un gatto*.

One of those moments you never forget. Pippo had gone upstairs to his flat lest he be drafted in to carry a suitcase. I went to the back of the van to unload our things. C went inside to inspect the new place. There was a pause, a pregnant silence. A car passed by. Grazia heaved at a suitcase and swore. Then there came a sound – a shriek, a wail, a howl of protest – from within the building.

*'Porca miseria!'* said Grazia.

Above our heads the french window was flung open. C stood on the edge of the abyss, her eyes wild.

'Don't jump!' I cried.

'Jump? It's that pig who'll jump!' she shouted down. 'The wiring still hasn't been done!'

C is a girl of determination rather than resignation: within seconds she was hammering on the door of the flat upstairs. Within five minutes the Alfa was howling back to the village, within fifteen it had returned with the sullen Romano. He had a canvas bag with him and reels of wire, not a single strand of which was the correct colour. I didn't even try to protest about this. My mind was already fully Italianate on the point. What the blazes did the colour of the insulation matter as long as the current flowed merrily along? But something else did matter, a fact that only dawned on us slowly.

'But the walls have just been plastered,' I pointed out. It wasn't just that the wiring had not been done: when the flat was redecorated it had actually been *forgotten*.

''*Fa niente.*'

'What do you mean, it doesn't matter?'

'We'll put the wires on the outside. It'll be fine. You'll see.'

I looked at C. 'Is he serious?'

'He's serious.' There wasn't any point in protesting, of course, not unless we were prepared to mount a major assault. The easiest thing was another Italian shrug. It is frequently the easiest thing. It explains many of the country's delights, but also some of its major ills. So we shrugged, and stowed our suitcases, and watched Romano get down to work. It was a terrifying experience. He went downstairs with a reel of wire, opened the box where the meters were, and connected the wire to the points. Then he came back up the stairs unreeling the wire as he went. At no point in this operation had he actually turned off the electricity supply. Blithely he shook out festoons of wire into the *ingresso* of our flat.

'That's all live,' I whispered. I pulled C back into the sanctuary of the bedroom. Like witnesses to a firework display we watched the rest of the performance from well back.

In England much used to be said about lack of physical courage on the part of the Italians. The main reason for this is that the English have too often equated physical courage with blind obedience of insane orders. What, an Italian would ask, what *purpose* is served by going over the top and walking into a wall of machine-gun fire? Italians are not only fatalists, they are also realists. It takes them no time at all to understand what British historians only stumble on half a century later, that the generals who order you to do things like that are fools and have got it all wrong.

None of this kind of absurdity has anything to do with what the Italian understands by the term courage. Their reluctance to be stupid is not a sign of cowardice. No, given something with purpose and, preferably, a bit of style, the Italian is amongst the most courageous on earth. That is why he drives the way he does (here the purpose is actually the style – the desire to arrive sooner is very secondary). But that is also why in 1941 their frogmen were prepared to climb aboard overgrown torpedoes and set off to war unprotected, in the dark, into the middle of enemy harbours to sink battleships. That is why, by late 1944 when the war in the peninsula was very far from over, there were some eighty thousand men and women under arms in *la Resistenza*. That is why Romano wired the entire kitchen and living room live.

His screwdriver spat like a snake. Blue sparks lit the place up like a discothèque.

'Is that safe?' I cried. 'For God's sake, you'll kill yourself!'

For the first time I saw Romano smile. '*Niente,*' he said. Nothing. His screwdriver sparked again and he snatched his hand away, shaking his fingers and blowing on them as though to put out a fire. 'It's quicker like this. Don't have to keep switching the current on and off. Where do you want the wall plugs?'

So, in a shower of sparks, we moved in beneath Grazia and Pippo. We had, of course, moved out of the *centro storico* but we had not lost it. A short stroll along the road past Giuseppina's *alimentari* shop and the filling station brought us to the public garden where the children played. From here the road curved back on itself and led up to the Piazza Garibaldi and the main gate. It was exactly the kind of stroll one might wish to take in the evening, perhaps taking a short cut through the public garden to admire the Roman sarcophagi, which in any other country in the world would have been in the national museum, solemnly labelled with their provenance and date and a description of what was obvious to the onlooker – the beautifully carved garlands and funerary figures and sacrificial animals ranged round their sides. In Avea, as in many other Italian towns and villages, they were nothing more than a public utility, doing duty as drinking fountain and flower tubs, beside the odd Corinthian capital and fragmented funerary inscription.

Once through the park and back on to the road you join the *passeggiata*, the evening stroll. The occasional car threads its way through the crowd no faster than a donkey; in the *passeggiata* the pedestrian rules, and his presence is signalled by the thrum of conversation. The noise of a crowd talking is a wonderful sound, a rich complex of rhythms, a blend of strange and thrilling percussions. You never hear it in Britain. That realisation comes as something of a shock. That murmuring, that haunting sea sound in which a dozen assignations and covenants are being made and broken, a hundred stories are being told and retold, a thousand platitudes are being repeated and rewarmed (for banalities are uttered in foreign tongues no less often than in your own) – that thrilling sound is never, ever heard in England. In England crowds shout or applaud, but they never converse. Yet in Italy, except in the depths of winter, you hear the sound any evening when, arm in arm, people leave their houses for the evening stroll.

# 5

In the new *palazzo* there were other tenants. Below us lived
a medical student from Bergamo and his Belgian wife; across
the landing from our front door were Maddalena and her daughter. Maddalena was a mystery. She had an anxious, hunted
look, the look of a grazing herbivore forever sniffing the air
for hint of a predator, forever glancing anxiously over its
shoulder to see if some enemy was creeping closer downwind.
Her smile was the placatory smile of one who has been afraid.

'Her man's gone,' Pippo told us. He shrugged, as though
such things were of no account. 'Found someone better.'

What did *better* mean? Better-looking? Better at putting up
with abuse? Better at cooking? Better at conversation? Better
at making love? Who knows? There was just Maddalena and
her daughter and her fear. Grazia used her as a kind of skivvy,
ordering her around in a manner which you might hesitate to
use with a dog: between landlady and tenant there was an
almost feudal sense of obligation and deference, of rights
claimed and rights granted. Chatelaine and vassal. One
guessed, correctly, that Maddalena was far behind with the
rent.

The medical student and his wife were very different. Margaret was a graduate from the University of Louvain in Belgium, while Ugo had won a place to read medicine at the
Catholic University in Rome. In Italy students are expected
to commute from home to the university in the nearest city
and there are no grants to help students from Bergamo who
are talented enough to win a place at one of the country's chief
medical schools, still less students who wish to get married.

Yet one does not turn down a place at one of the best medical schools, and one does not turn down the girl you love, and so there they were, living in penury in Avea, with Margaret taking odd jobs to scratch some kind of living for the two of them. Because her degree was not recognised in Italy, often enough the odd jobs were cleaning houses.

Neither Grazia nor Pippo were impressed by people who cleaned houses. They couldn't see a girl who spoke native English (her father had come from Liverpool), native Flemish, native French, fluent Italian, and had a degree in Geography from Belgium's premier University: all they could see was a girl who cleaned houses. She might be, at different times and to different people, Magaret, Marguerite, Magriet, Margarita, but to Grazia she was, like Maddalena, a skivvy.

Thus installed below Pippo and Grazia, allied with Ugo and Margaret, exchanging oblique nods with the anxious Maddalena, we began to establish our home. We were like nomads settling down for the first time, cautious in our purchases of the paraphernalia of married life, suspicious of possessions. But when you take an unfurnished flat in Italy it is *unfurnished*. Bare wires poke out of the ceiling; dumb pipes protrude from the walls. You feel lucky they have put the windows in.

In company with Grazia and her van we made the necessary purchases – 'I know where I can get them cheap. You come along with me. I'll not let the bastards cheat you.' And she was as good as her word. We bought a stove fired by a calorgas cylinder and a refrigerator; we were given a sink for the kitchen (Grazia had already leant us a bed) and found some cheap kitchen cupboards. Cane furniture, sold from stalls at the roadside, was the solution to many problems – comfortable chairs, living-room tables, shelving, lamps, all cane. And we bought a car. Lorenzo Colasanti helped with that.

'I'll take you to see a friend of mine,' he said. 'He's a car dealer in Rome.'

'Not Maserati.'

'Not Maserati,' he assured us.

So we went to the city with him, feeling like country hicks. The traffic roared and flashed past the car showroom, and ground to stagnation a few streets away. On thick-pile carpets beneath concealed fluorescent lighting we looked over some models.

'Really we want something second-hand.'

There was a palpable cooling of interest. Perhaps such dealings were beneath the manager. Finally, putting his best face on things, Lorenzo's friend admitted that he did stock second-hand models. In fact, now he thought about it, he had a bargain for us, as good as new.

'*Occasione*,' he said, demonstrating it with panache. 'Three thousand miles on the clock, one owner, *immacolata*.'

*Immacolata*. The expression struck me. A few years earlier an Englishman living in Malta had wanted to advertise his car in the local paper. He dictated a similar description to the girl in the small-ads department: 'Twenty thousand miles, one owner, immaculate condition.'

'You can't put that,' she said.

'What can't I put?'

'Immaculate condition.'

'Why on earth not? It describes my car perfectly.'

'I'm sorry, we can't print it.'

'What do you mean, you can't print it? I'm paying for the advertisement and I insist you print it.'

'We can't.'

'I insist.'

'I'll have to get the manager.'

'The manager? This is absurd.'

But the wretched man was called and shown the offending draft. 'He wants to say that,' protested the girl. 'Immaculate condition.'

'What the devil's wrong with it?' the Englishman demanded.

'Wrong with it?' The manager drew himself up. 'You can't use those words for a car!'

'Why not? It *is* in immaculate condition. That's a perfect description of the car I wish to sell. You can come and see yourself.'

'It cannot be applied to a car,' the manager insisted. 'The words immaculate condition can only be applied to the Virgin Mary.'

I had laughed. I still laugh. I'll bet the same story is told in Dublin. But when I heard Lorenzo's friend use the word *immacolata* a small thrill ran down my spine because suddenly, I, a man from the Protestant north, understood the manager of the small-ads department of the Maltese newspaper. It was the first palpable step into feeling another language in the way I feel my own. I grasped not just the literal meaning of the word but its semantic power. *L'Immacolata*. The Madonna of the Immaculate Conception, an arcane piece of dogma misunderstood by so many; but an essential part of Mediterranean civilisation. And the story about the Englishman in Malta and his wretched advertisement suddenly took on a third dimension, as though a flat piece of glass had unexpectedly grown into a prism, still transmitting light, yes, but at the same time splintering it into its components. The Englishman suddenly looked wooden, clumsy, rather stupid.

Under Lorenzo's benevolent eye – 'You can trust him, he's an old friend of mine' – we purchased the car of immaculate condition, signing two years' worth of *cambiali* to do so.

'We can't draw up *cambiali* for more than a year ahead,' the salesman assured us with oily charm. 'So we have to put the second year's payments all together in the last one.'

A *cambiale* is a promissory note. It is a document of mediaeval aspect. I am sure that the Frescobaldi bank issued *cambiali* in the thirteenth century; they would already have had a fusty look about them when Lorenzo de' Medici was dealing on the Florence stock exchange in the fifteenth. They are covered in those curious wavy patterns that are printed on bank notes, the kind of underlining Queen Elizabeth I used beneath her signature. Maybe that's where she got the idea from. If there is the slightest default on a *cambiale*, then the production of the unpaid and expired note gives the creditor summary powers of arrest.

I looked with awe at the figure he was referring to. 'You mean I am promising to pay all *that* on the sixteenth of January next year?'

'No, no, no.' Of course not. He smiled sympathetically. 'Just before it falls due you come back to us, we tear it up and we divide the sum up between another twelve.'

'Can't we pay the money by standing order?' I asked C. 'What the hell's a standing order in Italian?'

She attempted a translation. '*Un ordine per pagamenti regolari*,' she tried. The salesman looked blank.

'We just agree to pay you the right amount each month,' I attempted to explain. 'From our bank. A system they use in England.'

He looked at us with pity. 'But what happens if you decide not to pay?'

'You take the car back.'

'But we don't want the car back.'

'And I go to prison.'

He smiled again, this time without sympathy. 'If you don't pay the *cambiali* you will go to prison also.'

I looked desperately at C. 'Are you sure this will work?'

'Do we have a choice?'

'You're not signing *your* life away.'

'I'll come and visit you in prison.'

Feeling like Faust in the grip of Mephistopheles, I picked up the pen, pulled the twelve documents towards me and, with a due sense of solemnity, signed my future away against, apparently, the collateral of my own freedom.

But when we climbed into the car all money worries were forgotten. It was the first time I had sat behind the wheel of a left-hand-drive car, the first time I had ever driven in Italy. Outside the glittering Aladdin's cave of the showroom it was now dusk. Traffic swirled by in a torrent of light and sound: thrilling anarchy faced me.

Italian driving has a bad press. In fact there is no more 'Italian' driving than there is 'an Italian': Roman driving, Neapolitan driving, Milanese driving, yes. Italian driving, no. To unite the disparate groups would be a task equal to that which faced Count Cavour and King Victor Emmanuel in uniting the country. In Rome they may drive at eighty kilometres an hour the wrong way down one-way streets or circumvent a blockage by going round it on the pavement or crash red traffic lights with cheerful insouciance, but in the country it is as different as a Fiat is from a Ferrari. In Avea the driving is of the donkey-cart variety: you bumble along, nodding at acquaintances, waving to relatives, stopping abruptly and winding down the window to talk with friends driving in the opposite direction. Cars pile up behind you, but you don't hurry. The traffic moves with the rhythm of village life. Throughout Italy the car is both the expression of one's personality and the epitome of one's *paese*: in Milan somewhat businesslike, in Naples swaggering and dangerous like a Camorra killer, in Rome bloody-minded and inventive. The only thing that unites it all is a sensation that you can do more or less as you like. Carved up one moment, you will be doing the carving up the next. Rarely is there any resentment, and while the cities are not for the faint-hearted (there are no faint hearts amongst the Italian people), elsewhere, on country roads, you can rediscover the joys of what used to be known in England as 'motoring', wandering for miles without encountering more than a tractor or a truckload of hay or a flock of sheep. At a time when the motorcar is beginning to look intrusive and selfish, this is an exhilarating experience. So C and I climbed into the new car and plunged into the maelstrom. As we swept through the darkness towards the sanctuary of Avea we felt a strange sensation of liberation.

*

57

Pippo, of course, is an expert on cars. He drives his raging Alfa Romeo as though trying to coat the streets of Avea with rubber. I have spoken of donkey carts. If most of the village drives with the donkey-cart mentality, then Pippo drives with the quadriga mentality. A quadriga was one of those four-horse racing chariots which hurled round the Circus Maximus, chopping careless rivals and spectators to pieces. And the raging Alfa wasn't all: 'I also own a Ferrari. And a Lamborghini.'

'Where are they?' I asked, only half-believing.

He stroked his moustache and gave that conspiratorial smile. 'In Holland.'

'In Holland?'

'Impounded by Dutch customs.'

'Dutch customs?' Naïvely I imagined some kind of illegal import of motor vehicles.

'Friends of mine borrowed them. The customs searched the cars. Full of drugs. Nothing to do with me, of course; I didn't even know they were going to Holland.'

'Fine friends.'

'From Naples.'

'Why don't you go and claim the cars?'

He smiled pityingly. It was the same smile of the car salesman when we had attempted to explain about standing orders. There was no answer.

Besides the raging Alfa Romeo, Pippo also owns three trucks. That is how he earns his money.

'I'll carry anything anywhere,' he boasted. I was tempted to ask whether the Ferrari and the Lamborghini had been part of the boast but I restrained myself. He also owned a combine harvester. This monster lay inert in the yard behind the new apartment block which he was building in the village. NEW HOLLAND, it proclaimed along its side. Its tyres were perished, its slab sides streaked with rust. Nettles and bindweed seemed determined to exact a grim and fitting revenge on it.

The morning after we had bought the new car he went down to give us the benefit of his wide experience.

'*Bella macchina*,' he said, smiling his conspiratorial smile. His pudgy hands stroked its gleaming, metallic-grey flanks.

'It is second-hand,' I admitted. 'But we couldn't really afford a brand new one.'

At the mention of second-hand, Pippo's face fell; then it brightened optimistically. 'Like a used woman,' he said. 'More experience.' He raised the bonnet and peered at the engine. There were further disappointments. 'Small engine, only one carburettor. No acceleration. And had a crash as well.' He pointed. 'New light fitting.'

Fingered and insulted, her morals somehow called into question, the new car had lost its gloss. Grazia tutted volubly when she heard about the purchase. 'You signed *cambiali*? *Porca miseria*.'

One evening a month later she was hammering on our door. 'Where were you this morning?'

'At work.'

'You were lucky. The *vigili* came round. There's an unpaid *cambiale* at the bank. I persuaded them you were good people, honest English people, but you've got to go round first thing in the morning and pay it or they'll send it back.' She tutted again. 'You should never have signed them. Lucky I knew the *vigile*.' Perhaps she had learned by experience from Pippo for he is prodigal with money. Sometimes indigent, at other times he is floating on a sea of liquidity. When in the latter state he will pull from his pocket a wad of grimy ten-thousand-lire notes as thick as a roll of lavatory paper and distribute money with magnificent largess; when in the former state he would ask us if we could see our way to paying that month's rent in advance. Soon after we moved into the flat he called C to help him with some business matters. She went up to the *piano nobile* with trepidation.

'What on earth can he want?'

'Go and see.'

'But how can I help?'

He led her into the kitchen and sat her down. A crumpled

59

letter was thrust into her hand. It was on company letterhead. 'What do you think of this?'

C read it through. 'They seem to want payment for some-thing.' She quoted the sum.

'What do they say it is for? I don't remember.' He half-glanced at the page as though to remind himself.

'*Pozzolana*?' C read. 'What's that?'

'*Pozzolana*, ah yes. They want payment for the *pozzolana*.'

'What's *pozzolana*?'

'Cement. A type of cement.' He waved his hand at the letter. Gold glittered. 'Can you write a reply? You have a typewriter?'

C shrugged. 'We've got one. What do you want me to say?'

'Tell them I'll pay next month. Tell them that.'

She went away with the commission. When she returned the next day with the draft reply, Grazia was also at home. Pippo glanced at the letter and nodded, then passed it to his wife. She read it through.

'What do you think?' he asked her.

'*Brava*,' Grazia said. 'It's good.'

He nodded. '*Brava*, isn't she? Knows Italian, English. *Brava*.'

'And Maltese.'

Pippo laughed. He was never very sure about Malta. 'And Maltese. We'll send it just as it is.'

'You must sign it first.'

'Of course.' He reached into his inside pocket and produced a gold pen. With elaborate care, like a surgeon preparing his instruments, he unscrewed the cap and laid it on the table, then turned the letter towards him. He wrote. His signature was florid and complex, like a piece of crude filigree, pregnant with curlicues and flourishes.

'There.'

Every month when we paid the rent C wrote out a receipt for him to sign and every time he would glance at it with the same cunning expression as when he had glanced at that letter. '*Brava*,' he would say each time. And there was always the

60

same hint of uncertainty in his tone, the same sense that he was looking for reassurance as he inscribed his painfully ornamental signature. The fact is that Pippo is illiterate.

Illiterate, periodically indigent, he is also periodically filthy. The period, we realised, was menstrual. At the start of every month he is immaculate: white silk suit – as though he is about to take first Holy Communion – silk shirt, silk display handkerchief, brown and white co-respondent shoes. He will also have been to the hairdresser: his shoulder-length hair is blow dried, his jowls are shaven, his moustache razor-sharp. In short, he is magnificent. We would tell him so.

'*Ma quanto sei bello, stamattina!*'

He would raise his chin like Mussolini. 'You think so?'

'*Che bella figura.*'

And he would preen and strut like a small, rotund turkey. The problem is that he then doesn't seem to do anything to preserve the *figura*. For the remainder of the month he inhabits that suit and those shoes. He doesn't shave, he doesn't tend his hair, apparently he doesn't even wash. By the month's end he is half-bearded, he wears impromptu dreadlocks, his suit is like something salvaged from a jumble sale. The display handkerchief has long vanished.

And then he disappears for a day, to reappear once more in immaculate splendour. And the cycle of decay and resurrection recommences.

Not long after moving in we decided to have all our neighbours to dinner, to return the hospitality we had received. Maddalena could not come, of course. She smiled nervously and claimed some obscure appointment. But the medic and his wife were delighted, and so too were Pippo and Grazia.

It was a curious occasion. Jovial and full of *bonhomie* on his own territory, Pippo was strangely uneasy off it. Despite our having made certain that he knew the date and the time he still arrived home late that evening, long after dark, long after the time we had agreed. Grazia came down to apologise.

'But are you coming?' we asked.

'Of course. Of course.' She disappeared upstairs once more. There was another long wait while their four tenants giggled and speculated round the table below. What could they be doing?

'Hiding the gold under the mattress,' was Ugo's suggestion.

'Having a quick supper in case the foreigners don't feed them enough,' was Margaret's.

But when they finally appeared they confounded our wildest speculations: they were both wearing their nightclothes. Some things I can explain, other things remain a complete mystery. It is thus with this event. What, in their curious and convoluted minds, was the significance of this gesture? – for gesture it surely was. What did they mean by it? I can see them now, standing at our front door like survivors from a shipwreck, dressed in pyjamas and nightdress and woolly dressing gowns, with slippers on their feet. Bizarre. Throughout the subsequent meal, a meal of suppressed hysteria, they kept disappearing upstairs on nameless and inexplicable errands. I still have no idea why. Worse, I cannot even invent an explanation that is at once coherent and satisfactory. Social anthropologists go off to Papua New Guinea or deepest Amazonia to study the mysterious rites of natives and end up discovering that, underneath the costume and the rituals, they are rather like us. But not Grazia and Pippo. And no anthropologist for miles.

Familiarity breeds not contempt but tolerance. Despite Pippo's eccentricities we had begun to feel at home. If we walked up to the old village, no longer did the old boys stop their talk and stare. Now they would nod and grin and call out *buon di*. If I went over I would be offered a glass of that cloudy wine – '*vino genuino*' – and taken into the conversation, to spend a few minutes bravely, hopelessly floundering around in the mire of dialect. Occasionally they would even invite me to take a hand of *scopa*.

Scopa is a broom, but it is also a ubiquitous game of cards, played with the ancient Italian deck whose suits are swords, coins, sticks, and cups. Antecedents of the modern suits – *spade*, *denari*, *bastoni*, *coppe* have become spades, diamonds, clubs and hearts – in northern Europe the original deck is only familiar as part of the Tarot pack, the kind of thing you buy in shops which sell joss sticks and horoscopes and books on transcendental meditation. But in Italy, however, they remain the ordinary playing cards, dog-eared things slapped down between the tumblers of wine, to the accompaniment of imprecations and shouts of anguish.

'*O professor*! *Venga a giocar, venga, venga,*' they would call and I would decline with what I hoped was grace. Even to watch a game of *scopa* is to partake in a short but deadly skirmish in which peaceable men are transformed into aggressive, blaspheming warriors. Rarely does anyone seem overjoyed by victory, rather they appear to relish the agonies of defeat. They swear when they lose the seven of *denari*, the *settebello*, and blast when their opponent makes the eponymous *scopa* and sweeps the table of cards. They curse a variety of deities, ancient and modern, for their ill luck and treat good fortune as though it is only their just deserts. *Per fortuna* is, of course, rather more than the empty ejaculation it may seen at first. Fortuna herself was an ancient Italic goddess introduced into Rome during the reign of one of the legendary kings, Servius Tullius. In and around Avea people must have been invoking the names of the goddess since, literally, time immemorial.

'You stand just there, *professor*,' Pippo insisted on one occasion. '*Mi porti la fortuna.*'

I hadn't noticed, but when you are playing your mind becomes attuned not only to the cards that have already gone (that is mere memory and mathematics) but also to the little things that influence the way the next ones fall, the precise arrangement of chairs, the position of glasses on the table, whether you have a handkerchief in your top pocket, all that kind of thing. Fortuna is a demanding and capricious deity.

'You stay just where you are, *professor*, and we'll take the whole lot,' he asserted.

Dutifully I froze. The cards flickered across the table into their piles. The imprecations began. Pippo lost the round disastrously.

It had all been my fault. As his opponent counted his winnings my landlord looked up at me with an expression full of reproach. I was a *iettatore*, a carrier of ill luck.

'I'd better go,' I suggested as they prepared to deal once more. Pippo did not argue. While climbing the steps to the bar I heard a great shout of triumph from behind me. Pippo had just taken the *settebello*. Fortuna had been appeased.

There were other games which one might play in the bar but there were many more that were banned. A long list of prohibitions hung on the wall beside the counter. It included *morra*.

'What's *morra*?' I asked.

64

Pippo winced at the mere mention and a grimy forefinger closed his lips. 'Shhh!'

Had I trespassed on some dark secret of village life, ritual child sacrifice perhaps? 'But what on earth *is* it?'

Taking me by the arm he led me outside, beyond the range of eavesdroppers. It all seemed too good to be true. Strip poker? Soliciting? One's imagination floundered.

'For God's sake, what is it?'

We were standing in the archway of the village gate, deep in the shadows. He huddled in a corner to demonstrate. 'You do this.' Without warning he stuck three fingers out at me. 'And the other fellow does the same, maybe one or two, who knows? Any number he likes, at exactly the same time. And at the same time he shouts the number. You know what I mean?'

I frowned, completely bewildered. 'What number?'

'He guesses. Your fingers and mine. What they all add up to.'

Understanding dawned. 'And if he guesses right . . .'

'He wins the money.'

'We used to play a game like that as children. Hic, Haec, Hoc, we used to say – that's Latin – and then you either make paper, stone or scissors.' I showed him. 'Paper wraps stone. Scissors cut paper. Stone blunts scissors. You see?' But he didn't really seem to care. 'So what's wrong with *morra*?' I asked. 'It sounds a good game to me. Difficult.'

'*Sai quando hanno ucciso Gesù?*' he whispered.

Surely I had misheard. 'What?'

'*Quando hanno ucciso Gesù,*' he repeated.

'When they killed Jesus?'

He nodded. 'You know about that?'

'I've heard tell.'

He glanced over his shoulder as though Roman soldiers might even now leap out of the shadows of the archway and take him away as well. 'They killed him on the cross, *mortacci loro*. You know that. And then they played a game.'

'A game?'

'A game.'

'Who played?'

'The soldiers, at the foot of the cross, *mortacci loro*. Well, that's the game they played. *Morra*.'

There is another game that is banned in the Bar Rasenna. It is right at the bottom of the list, far below *morra* and poker and craps and all other blasphemies. To be precise, it is number thirty-two. It is *pesca con gru magnetica*, fishing with a magnetic hook. I didn't even bother to ask.

# 6

Throughout November, in the clarity of autumn evenings, the village cemetery glimmers with candlelight, a myriad of stars flickering around the graves in a *festa* for the dead. Seeing the lights it is easy to believe, as the Romans did, that the dead are set in the heavens. Every evening onwards from All Souls day, *il giorno dei morti*, families make their way from Avea to the graves of their relatives, carrying flowers and candles, carrying prayers and memories. Grazia's flower shop works at treble time: vases of yellow and white chrysanthemums crowd the little square.

It is a constant throughout the peninsula: people travel hundreds of miles to be back in their own *paese* on the second of November to visit their family graves. In the cities the public bus companies lay on special services. In Venice extra *vaporetti* ply at no charge between the Fondamenta Nuova and the cemetery island of San Michele. The pilgrim groups are not gloomy. Children laugh and chase one another. The adults gossip. But there is an underlying solemnity about the event which carries with it something of the original meaning of that word – it is ritual and necessary, simply the thing you do and always have done.

Doubtless it was much the same with the Etruscans. Only for the dead did the Etruscans build to last and so it is through their tombs and necropolises that we know them best. Everything else they built of wood. Even their temples, though they had stone foundations and footings, were wooden, brightly decorated with painted terracotta. If you want a mental image of an Etruscan temple, don't imagine something on the lines of the Parthenon: a Chinese pagoda or a Japanese Shinto shrine would be nearer the mark. Wide wooden eaves overhang the stone base. Lurid devils leer and gibber at the onlooker. A statue of the god strides along the ridge of the roof. But apart from some of the terracotta fitments, not a single example remains to us; it is the necropolis we are familiar with, the city of the dead built on a convenient hill just outside the town, a small city of tombs with doors opening out on to carefully laid-out streets. It was so then, it is so now: like all Italian villages Avea's *campo santo*, lying on the outskirts of the place, is a necropolis, a small walled village with a chapel at the head and narrow alleyways between the tombs. The dead are enshrined in family mausoleums or posted in little cubicles in the walls. Their photographs on the outside, carefully plasticised, stare solemnly out at the future they never saw. In ancient times it was not dissimilar: Cerveteri's famous Etruscan necropolis is a veritable city of the dead, and in the woods to the north of Veii there is a *columbarium*, 'dove cot', where the cinerary urns were posted just like the coffin cubicles of Avea's cemetery. And doubtless Etruscan families made their way from the city of the living to the city of the dead, bearing offerings and candles, and mixed memories.

'Come and see,' said Pia when the subject came up one evening when we were round at her house. She unfolded herself from the sofa and took a bunch of keys down from a hook. We followed her through a door from the kitchen and down narrow curling stairs into the cellars of the house, into the bowels of the village itself. Beyond a further door the walls turned from *tufo* blocks into diagonally laid brick – 'Roman,' she said carelessly – and, as we went down a passage, from brick into raw, carved rock. The air was cold. Pia's rich and aggressive perfume fought a losing battle with the sour smell of damp. Further on we found ourselves at a blind ending. In the light from a single bulb we could see two shallow troughs on either side. They were exactly the size for a human body.

'Etruscan, we think. Of course there was nothing else.'

'You think? Didn't you get anyone in to have a look?'

Pia regarded me pityingly. 'The Soprintendenza? They would have suspended all work for ten years. We just asked Franco the builder not to disturb anything and to put a door up. He knew what he was doing.' She shrugged. 'What else could we do?'

I couldn't really answer that. The puritan mind says call the archaeologists, but then the puritan mind is northern European, where the problem does not arise in quite so acute or domestic a form. And anyway, I consoled myself, puritans are hardly the people to entrust with treasures.

I looked for decoration on the wall but found only chisel marks. Was it a poor tomb, then? How many others lay beneath the mediaeval buildings of Avea? I wondered. How many complete with grave goods and carvings? Such questions become commonplace in Italy, almost banal. What else lies beneath the present city of Rome? What exactly did Mussolini cover up with the Via dei Fori Imperiali, his triumphal way from Piazza Venezia to the Colosseum? What lies beneath Saint Peter's (Pope Pius XII had the power and interest to attempt to satisfy that one), or beneath Saint John Lateran, or beneath the buildings that now sit in the arc of Pompey's theatre? The speculations are endless. Not far from Avea a large dual carriageway has a nerve-racking chicane built into it where the road-workers uncovered a Roman villa while they were widening the old road. Polychrome mosaics have been unearthed. Now, while the authorities decide what to do about them, the mosaics are carefully covered with plastic and roofed over with corrugated iron. The chicane, where the road narrows for a hundred yards from near *autostrada* to its original two-way traffic, is an authentic road-safety nightmare. To my certain knowledge it has been like that for fifteen years.

Pia put out a hand and touched my arm. 'It's cold. Let's go back.'

C invited me to go first. Perhaps she did not want to leave

me behind in the shadows with Pia. I went back up the stairs feeling like Orpheus emerging from Hades, except that I had two Eurydices, and no singing voice worth mentioning.

Something Pia said on that occasion only made sense some time after. She had remarked of Franco the *muratore*, 'He knew what he was doing'. But it wasn't until later that we discovered what she meant.

November is not only the month of the dead, it is also the month of the olive harvest. Oreste invited us to come and watch . . . and maybe help. His field was over the hill from the village, beyond the *campo santo* with its glimmering candles, a half-hour's walk away. The *contadini* have always lived like this, returning every evening from the fields to the security of the village.

'Until the war they used to shut the gate,' he told us. 'I came back from Russia to find the gate open, the girls walking out with the boys after dark, all kinds of stuff!' He roared with laughter and nodded in the direction of his wife. 'In our day I wasn't allowed to speak to her without her aunt there. Never saw her neck until the wedding night . . . and then' – he indicated yards of drapery around his own diminutive body – 'a *camicia* as long as the Pope's *sottana*. Maybe if they'd let me look at her first I wouldn't have married her!'

This pattern of daily migration to and from the fields is why there are so few old houses in the countryside itself; and it smacks, I suspect, of a countryside that was barely safe until the nineteenth century. Every morning before dawn the gate would be opened and the men and women would emerge into the half-light, stumping out into a land that was viewed with mixed emotions – half as a vital source of food, half as a fount of all their misery. Oreste had left this world behind him when he went away to war, and he returned from the Russia of the collective farms and the prison camps to find all had changed: he now owned the fields he had worked or could hire them from the Università, the agency founded by the *comune* to hold land on behalf of the labourers. But the Italian countryman is a conservative creature. To watch Oreste in brown corduroy trousers and grey woollen vest and battered jacket setting out to his fields with one of the last working donkeys of the village, you would not have believed anything had changed from the eighteenth century.

The donkey was the usual grimly determined brute, capable of bearing unreasonable loads when in a good mood, possessed of human fits of malignity when not. It was known as *la bestia*, the beast. Frequently its principal load was Oreste's wife Lucia, seated side-saddle on a pile of fodder or a sack of grain, rocking and swaying with the motion while Oreste himself staggered along leading *la bestia* by a piece of rope. We followed them on the *motorino*, a form of transport markedly more capricious than *la bestia*.

On this occasion Lucia carried an armful of chrysanthemums from Grazia's flower shop. First stop, of course, was the cemetery. They knew every occupant, were related to most. As though addressing words of greeting to the staring faces of the dead, the old couple nodded and muttered their way along the lanes.

'Old Romano, bless his soul. A fine man, courted the doctor's daughter but she went off with that fellow from Sutri. Then there's Elena – you remember Elena, the one that married Giovanni's son? Her children went to America. And the

71

de Santis father and son, that was a terrible thing. He was married to my cousin . . .' And so it went on, until finally we were at his own family plot and ALFONSO BUONAROTTI was staring out of his little oval of plastic with an expression of mingled surprise and suspicion. Alongside was the blurred but surprisingly youthful face of MARIA CONCETTA BUONAROTTI, NATA DI LORENZO. CARISSIMA MOGLIE DI ALFONSO, and something of the story was there in the dates: Alfonso died in 1953, two years after Oreste's return from Russia; but his wife, Oreste's mother, had died in 1913.

'*Tisi*,' the old man said, nodding towards his mother's picture and crossing himself. 'I was eight years old.' He smiled his gap-toothed smile. 'I hardly remember her. Just her smell, and' – he put his hands to his shoulders – 'the feel of her.'

*Tisi* is phthisis, tuberculosis.

'*Babbo* never remarried. He always said that a part of him had died with her. Who knows?'

Votive candles glimmered palely in the bright sunshine. Lucia went down on her knees to remove a mass of fading flowers from the metal vase and replace them with the new bunch. We stood a moment over this little echo of the past, then filed out of the *campo santo* into the present. The olive harvest waited.

In Oreste's field a tracery of vines hung between the olives. They looked like staunch and sober citizens supporting reeling drunks. *Coltura promiscua*, promiscuous cultivation, is the delightful name for this interplanting of olive and vine. It is frowned upon by modern producers of both wine and oil but is still much practised round Avea. It is the result of hedging your bets against failure, a typical precaution of the sharecropper. Oreste had a little hut and greenhouse in one corner of the field. A body panel of a Fiat 500 had been built into the wall so you opened an incongruous car door in order to step into the warm, green atmosphere. He struggled back out with a long ladder and a bundle of netting, refusing all offers of help. For all his crooked legs Oreste was a tireless worker. The netting was hung from the branches and, to Lucia's cries of encouragement and warning, up he went into the crown of the trees and laid about him with a short-handled rake to drag the fruit down. It would have been an impressive display for any man in his seventies; for someone who had been crippled by the Russian winter and spent nine years in prison camps it was nothing short of heroic.

We spent some time helping Lucia gather up the fruit into baskets for transport to the press, and later we sat with them and ate the food we had brought – what C referred to in her own language as *hobz biz-zejt*. This is the universal food of the Mediterranean peasant – bread and oil rubbed with tomatoes. The dead seemed far away. With the *vendemmia* over, the vine leaves had turned to gold and rust, but the olive leaves which shaded them were eternal, flickering silver and green in the breeze, symbols of many things – prosperity, peace, salvation, amongst others. Contrary to the words of scripture, in Italy it is not palm fronds which are held aloft by the faithful outside the church on Palm Sunday, but olive branches. Maybe that's it – the month of the dead is also the month of the olive, the symbol of hope.

In the evening the panniers were loaded on to *la bestia* and we made our way back to the village. The olives would go to the *frantoio*, the press, where twin grindstones march round and round in a tub and render the fruit down to a pulp. The pressing of the olives and the extraction of the oil must be done cold. The oil is a heavy, cloudy liquid, green like bottle glass and freezing semi-solid in the cold of winter. It has low acidity and there is no chemical treatment used. Something you might buy on the supermarket shelf, even in these enlightened times, is a feeble and anaemic thing by comparison, but even then you can come near: *olio extra vergine* has the lowest acid content of all (less than 1 per cent), *olio vergine* is more acid (1–2 per cent), *olio di oliva* (beware, because strictly speaking the term olive oil, which seems generic, is actually

73

specific to this third grade) is a mixture of *vergine* with refined olive oil which has been extracted hot and is chemically treated to reduce its acidity; and finally there is *olio di sansa di oliva*, a mixture of *olio vergine* with oil which has been extracted from the pulp by the use of organic solvents. At this end of the spectrum of oils, from the deep green of *extra vergine* one has arrived at a pale straw colour.

The evening after our efforts at the olive harvest we went round to Oreste's for supper and in celebration of our labours Lucia made *bruschetta* – bread toasted over the wood fire in the corner of her kitchen, then rubbed with a clove of Oreste's garlic – a clove like the knuckle of a heavy-weight boxer – before being soaked in oil and seasoned with pepper and salt. You may spread it, as Lucia did, with chopped tomatoes and fresh basil leaves. Of course it is just C's *hobz biz-zejt* under another guise, but as always with the finest food the subtle variations are important.

'*Siete quasi contadini!*' cried Oreste, raising his glass and roaring with laughter at the idea. You are almost peasants. It was a fine compliment.

It was one day in December with an edge of frost on the air and the scent of snow coming down from the mountains that C and I found the tomb. During the early morning there had been a luminous mist hanging over the village but by ten o'clock the sun had eaten into it like acid dissolving away pearl. Behind the pearl was a sky the precise and flawless colour of turquoise. We went to explore the countryside north of Veii, a patchwork of cultivated fields and small copses, of curious humps and bulges and the occasional opening into an empty cave. Along our path there was a small copse of oak and just beyond it we found ourselves on the edge of an expanse of fresh plough. A *Carabinieri* patrol car and a van were parked by the gate. The van bore the legend SOPRINTEN-DENZA ARCHEOLOGICA PER ETRURIA MERIDIONALE. A path of beaten earth led across the

74

plough to the rising ground at the far edge of the field where men were digging.

Understanding dawned. 'They were saying something about it in the village this morning,' C remarked. 'You know that *muratore* who works for Pia? Franco, his name is. She mentioned him. He was in the *alimentari* and he said something about a tomb but I thought he was talking about the cemetery. I thought he mentioned the police . . .'

We picked our way across the makeshift path to have a look. Against the bank on the edge of the field was a large pit almost six feet deep. Excavated earth was banked up beside it. Two *carabinieri*, resplendent in black and silver and red, looked up as we came over. They quickly decided we were of no consequence and turned back to the activity in the bottom of the pit.

'*Tombaroli*,' the foreman told us when we asked what had happened. Tomb robbers. 'The *guardia* surprised them last night. And once they've started we have to excavate the whole thing, otherwise they'll come back to finish the job.'

He had half a dozen men working under him, labouring with spades at the bottom of the pit. They looked more like men on a building site than workers for the archaeology department, but in overall charge was a young girl in dungarees who just couldn't have been a navvy.

'*La dottoressa*,' the foreman explained in awed tones. She was crouching on the rim of the hole, pointing and giving instructions. She barely accorded us a glance. One presumed that unlike Pippo she was actually entitled to her doctorate.

The foreman pointed. 'There's the entrance.' At the bottom of the pit there were brown steps leading down into the earth.

The dungareed archaeologist called for the men to go slowly.

'How did they know it was here?' I asked the foreman.

He shrugged. 'Oh, they have ways, instruments some of them. And there's more of them than us.'

'How long will it take you?'

75

'A few hours. If we don't finish today we'll have to put a guard over it during the night and come back first thing tomorrow.'

'And what do you do at the end?'

He shrugged. 'At the end? We take out anything of interest, seal the tomb up again and put all the earth back. What else can you do?'

'The things go into a museum?'

'A museum?' He laughed. 'The museums are already full of stuff.' *Robaccia*, he said: rubbish. 'Unless it is very special, anything we find just goes into store. Once the archaeologists have had a look at it.'

We watched for a bit more and then wandered off. Some time later we came back to find them working away at a stone block at the foot of the stairs. There was none of the drama one might have expected, nothing about it that smacked of Howard Carter at the tomb of Tutankhamun. There was a bit of grunting and subdued cursing – '*Porca matosca*,' one of the workmen muttered, using the euphemism to avoid hurting the *dottoressa*'s sensibilities (the actual phrase is *porca madonna*) – and eventually the entrance stone was manoeuvred out of the way. There was just a black hole. The archaeologist looked up from her notebook.

'*Pronto?*' The workmen stood aside for her and she climbed down and crouched at the entrance with a flashlight. We imagined skeletons, pots, the dull gleam of gold.

'*Vuoto*,' she said laconically. Empty. Just to make certain she went down on her knees and crawled part way in, leaving her denim-clad backside out in the light. One of the workmen grinned and raised his eyebrows, but the others were unmoved. *La dottoressa* was apparently not to be trifled with. Eventually she backed out, soil on her hands and knees. '*Vuoto*,' she repeated, brushing herself down.

'They usually are,' the foreman observed. As the *dottoressa* climbed out of the pit he began to marshal his labourers for the dispiriting task of undoing what they had just done. There were no complaints. It was a job of work.

'Why was it empty?' I asked the archaeologist as she passed by. She looked at us indifferently, brushing stray hair aside with her forearm. 'Who knows? They've been robbing them for centuries. The Romans started it. It could have been anyone.'

The labourers were heaving the entrance stone back into position. The *carabinieri* had gone back to their patrol car. *La dottoressa* walked away towards the van. She seemed a curiously modern figure amongst the traces of an extinct civilisation.

# 7

The sequel to the discovery of the tomb came much later. It was not a literal sequel, but in a very definite sense it was a moral one: while watching the fruitless piece of rescue archaeology being carried out by the Soprintendenza, I had been in some sense on the side of the angels. In the sequel I was on the side of the devils. The experience, the specific duality of it, is peculiarly Italian because in Italy the divide between morality and legality may be very wide indeed. Italians are no less moral than the English but they are very much less legal, and whereas an Englishman might go through life doing nothing more criminal than smuggling a little extra duty-free

through customs, rare is the Italian who will not, quite unabashed, treat a whole range of legislation with cavalier aban-
don. It is a tradition founded on an in-built suspicion of
government, a conviction, a perfectly understandable conviction, that most of the money the government does collect will
be wasted. The politicians are not fools – every Italian will
admit that they are the most cunning of all, dwelling in an
ivory tower that is both impregnable and luxurious – but they
are not admirable. They are, in fact, a disgrace to the nation.
And the entire nation knows that any money that gets into the
hands of the government will either go into peoples' pockets,
or go to pay moonlighting bureaucrats (there's another whole
sector of society quietly bending the rules) – or simply go
down the drain. So every firm and not a few private individuals
employ 'tax consultants' who actually are placemen in the tax
departments. Their consultancy involves nothing more than
keeping things quiet for their employers. This is neither
remarkable nor sensational; it is just normal, the way things
work. And of course it is not considered immoral.

A similar attitude holds for such an arcane matter as tomb
robbing.

By the time of the sequel, by the time I found myself on
the side of the devils, we had moved with Grazia and Pippo
to their new *palazzo* nearer the *centro storico*. Work was still
being done on the upper storey – work was always being done
on the upper storey – and when we were called in for a coffee
by Grazia one morning we found Franco the *muratore* sitting
at the kitchen table. His hands were grey with cement dust
and like all of his trade he had made a hat out of that morning's
newspaper, a neatly folded box like the carpenter's hat in the
Tenniel illustrations for *Through the Looking Glass*.

'*Piacere*,' he said, nodding in some kind of recognition.
'You're friends of Signora Colasanti,' he added, as though to
place us.

'And you're the *muratore* who opened up the tomb in her
cellar,' I said.

He displayed the usual set of brown teeth.

Grazia shrieked with laughter. 'That's his job,' she said. 'He makes more by robbing tombs than building walls.'

Franco protested innocence.

'You want to see?' she asked me, as though determined to prove her point. 'Go on, get that stuff' – *quella robaccia* – 'you showed me. Go!'

He rubbed his face reflectively. 'It's better not. Better not to carry it round.'

'*Mortacci tuoi*!' she yelled at him. 'Go and get it! What are you afraid of, *gli sbirri*?' *Gli sbirri* are the cops. Reluctantly Franco got to his feet and went out. He was gone about fifteen minutes and when he returned he was carrying something wrapped in a piece of old newspaper, a bit of plumbing perhaps.

'*Ecco*,' he said, putting the package carefully on the table. His grimy thumbs unwrapped the package and disclosed, in the midst of Grazia's kitchen table, a small black pot. '*Bucchero*,' he said.

*Bucchero* was a peculiarly Etruscan pottery technique. The pots were made with a clay rich in iron oxide and they were fired in a reducing, oxygen-starved kiln. The oxide is thus chemically reduced to iron to produce the black, metallic effect. This was a cup about fifteen centimetres high with a thick stem and two handles – a kylix, I suppose, although it was rather narrower than the classic form. But for a chip in the rim it was perfect.

'Is it genuine?' I asked absurdly.

He laughed. 'It's a bargain.' But he wasn't offering it to us, or if he was he had an over-optimistic idea of the financial resources of *gli stranieri*. 'One million lire,' he said. At the rate of exchange at that time it worked out at about five hundred and fifty pounds.

'Robbery!' exclaimed Grazia.

Franco nodded. 'That's right.'

We sat there contemplating this little piece of Italy's prehistory. It gleamed like polished iron and there was something impish about it, as though it knew its own sly, secret power. I wondered whether I was on the side of the devils or the angels. If this little pot had been found by the authoritative *dottoressa* it would have been glanced at, labelled with its provenance, possibly (but not very probably) dated by a thermoluminescence test, and then put away in a storeroom of the Villa Giulia along with a thousand others just like it. But it had been found by Franco, and here it was sitting on a kitchen table and enchanting even those who couldn't afford it by its heavy, pewter gleam. And someone who liked it would buy it and it would sit in a cabinet, possibly with a small spotlight on it, and dinner guests – maybe the local mayor or the *capitano* of Carabinieri – would admire it. Who were the devils?

'Where did you find it?' I asked.

Franco smiled into his moustache.

'He'll not say a word,' said Grazia.

'We saw the Soprintendenza opening a tomb a few months ago.' I told him the location and he nodded. There was a gleam of amusement in his eyes.

'Was it you who found it?'

'*Può darsi.*' Could be.

'How do you find them?'

He rubbed his chin thoughtfully. 'Experience,' he said. 'And a little skill.' And slowly he began to explain, talking of knowing the lie of the land and sensing vibrations and resonances, and using sounding rods and drills, *trivelli*. It seemed to be a curious mixture of the occult and the scientific, like water divining. 'And there are some who use electronic instruments' – he made a face – 'but not me. I prefer the traditional methods.'

'And when you open your next tomb,' I said, 'can you take me along with you?'

He looked silently at me for a while. '*Non è un gioco*,' he said.

'I know it's not a game,' I replied.

\*

I left it at that, not knowing how my request had gone down. It came as something of a surprise when, encountering Franco in the bar by the main gate some days later, he smiled into his moustache and asked me whether I was still interested. I hadn't really thought about it. I even had to pause for a moment before I realised what he was talking about.

'Of course.'

'Then we're doing something tonight.'

'Tonight? That's rather short notice.'

He shrugged. Take it or leave it. 'Signor Colasanti's coming.'

Maybe that tipped the balance. 'Okay, tonight.'

'I'll be outside the *palazzo* at eleven o'clock. It'll be cold.'

'Eleven o'clock.'

C was not amused. 'You can't leave me like this and go wandering round the countryside at night. You might get arrested.'

'Franco's never been arrested.'

'It's not fair.'

'And I'll never have another opportunity. You don't get asked twice to go on this sort of thing.'

She agreed reluctantly. When evening came I was ready, clad in a thick sweater and anorak, and feeling like a thief about to set off on some housebreaking job. But when the car finally pulled up outside there was a distinct air of tourist trip about the whole thing. Other faces peered and grinned at me as I climbed in and introductions were made. In the finest tradition of cheap thrillers I was referred to as *l'inglese* – as it might have been The Sicilian in a gangster film or The Virginian in a western. The other two did not seem to be a very illegal pair at all. One I recognised as a cashier in the bank, the other revealed himself as a colleague of Lorenzo. Apparently Lorenzo himself was in the car following. So we set off, more like a group going off for a fishing expedition than a band of men bent on robbing tombs. In the prevailing spirit of jocularity I tried to tell them about the resurrectionists of nineteenth-century England, who used to snatch fresh corpses to sell them for dissection. The attempt was a dismal failure. They seemed to think I was talking about something that happened nowadays – they were perfectly willing to accept the idea – and by the time that misunderstanding had been cleared up they couldn't see the point of the story.

'I feel a bit like Jerry Cruncher,' I explained. Even as I uttered the name I sensed the whole conversation running out of control. 'He robbed graves, you see. For bodies, not pots. I feel a bit like him . . .'

'*Vero?*' they asked. Really? There was a suggestion of patience about their tone, the patience of the psychiatrist.

'He wasn't real. But they were like that, these resurrectionists.' I had hazarded the word *resurrezionisti*. 'He was a character in . . .' but too late I realised that I didn't know the title of the book in Italian and they had probably not even heard of Dickens anyway. '*Una storia di due città,*' I guessed. 'A novel by Dickens. You know Dickens, Charles Dickens?' I even gave the name a kind of Italian flavour – Charlesa Deekensa.

The silence in the little car was profound. They had not heard of Charlesa Deekensa. They had no idea what the two cities had to do with it. They were more than ever convinced that foreigners were eccentric.

'How long?' asked someone after an eternity.

'A few minutes,' replied Franco.

We slowed down and turned off the road, bumping along a track before coming to a halt in the middle of the countryside somewhere, I guessed, near Sutri. There were no lights visible, just the glimmer of torches and the looming shadows of trees. Beyond the trees a dark hillside shut out a segment of the night sky.

Franco and his mate were pulling tools from the boots of the two cars – spades and pickaxes, some rope, half a dozen lamps. He distributed them amongst us and then urged us forward. '*Avanti! È silenzio!*'

83

One person remained with the cars. The rest of us, Jerry Cruncher and his mates by Charlesa Deekensa, set off into the woods carrying the motley assortment of excavation gear. Somewhere in the distance a dog barked. We walked for some time, blundering through undergrowth, breaking out on to a moonlit hillside for a while, then down into the woods again. By the time Franco called a halt I had completely lost all sense of direction. We dumped the equipment in a heap beside a clump of brambles and turned the lamps on. Shadows reared and loomed around us, drawing the darkness in. There was a bit of nervous joking.

'It's just like military service,' someone remarked.

'You mean we really are lost?' Lorenzo asked. The laughter was hushed to silence.

'Where's the damned tomb then?'

'You're standing on it.'

There was nothing but a slight rise in the ground, but when Franco jumped you could feel something, a curious resonance in the earth as though we were standing on a drum. 'We begin there,' he said, indicating the base of the mound. 'That is where the entrance should be.'

Someone began to wield a spade. Lorenzo swung the pickaxe and levered a rock out of the way.

'Keep it quiet,' someone urged.

'How can I keep a pickaxe quiet?'

Franco's friend went back up the hill to keep watch. 'The track's over there,' Franco told him. 'Look for car lights moving along it. And listen for the sound of Gino's horn. He'll sound a warning if anyone comes.'

I was definitely on the side of the devils. I took up a spade and began to work at the pit. The pile of fresh soil grew. I thought of the *dottoressa* in her dungarees, and what she'd have thought . . .

'Hey!'

The shout came from the top of the hill. 'Who is it?'

'Lights!'

84

'Jesus, put those lamps out!'

'What is it?'

Someone ran down the hill. 'Lights!' he called. 'On the road.'

'*Polizia*!' Who first whispered it was never clear but once uttered it was repeated, and once repeated it was the truth. '*Polizia*!'

'Jesus!'

Shadows scattered in the moonlight, dropping spades and picks, running for the trees.

'Over here!'

'*Polizia*!'

'Get out of it!'

There was a desperate scrambling and then a sudden silence around us, just the noise of the trees and the faint scurrying of the undergrowth. Somewhere in the distance someone went crashing through the wood.

'*Chi c'è?*'

With a wave of relief I recognised Lorenzo's voice. I called quietly to him and he crawled over.

'What happened?'

'Have they gone?'

'Who?'

'The *polizia*.'

'I've no idea. I didn't see them.'

'Two of them. I could see their hats.'

'Shhh.'

We crouched amongst the trees and peered helplessly into the darkness. Shadows moved at our command. A hedgehog rooting somewhere nearby became a *brigadiere* of *Carabinieri* creeping up on us. The distant bark of a fox was a police dog working through the undergrowth. The loudest thing in my whole, disorientated world was the pounding of my heart.

How long we stayed like that I don't know but eventually Lorenzo whispered, 'Shall we go? I think they've missed us.'

'Go where?'

'Back to the cars.'

'Where are the cars?'

'Over the hill.'

We began to move. Davy Crockett would have been proud of us. Jumping at shadows and lying low for minutes on end, we worked our way round the hill and down through the trees. At one point I stopped and called for silence.

'I can hear a car engine.'

We waited a moment, then crept on.

'Lights, headlights,' Lorenzo said after a while.

We crept forward to the edge of the trees, expecting to see blue lamps flashing, men in uniform standing around, companions in handcuffs. But there was just one car waiting on the track with its engine running and its lights on. I recognised Franco sitting at the wheel.

'Where the devil were you?'

'What happened? Where are the police?'

'The police? There weren't any police.'

'No police?'

'No police.'

'What was it, then? Where are the others?'

'They've gone. There was no point waiting. For God's sake get in and let's go.'

'But what was it?'

He put the car into gear and pulled away from the roadside even before we had shut the doors. 'It was that idiot who went up to the top of the hill, your colleague, what's his name?'

'Daniele.'

'Daniele. He saw lights on the road.'

'Well, then.'

'There were no police. They were just the lights of this car.'

'But Daniele never said police. He just said lights.'

'Someone said police.'

'Well, it wasn't Daniele.'

We argued about it all the way back to the village. As we

arrived, dawn was just breaking. C was already awake . . . or maybe she hadn't ever been asleep.

'Just like children,' was her judgement of the matter.

So no actual sin had been committed, no collection of antiquities despoiled, but then it is intention rather than commission that constitutes the sin. As I sat down to breakfast I reflected that Jerry Cruncher had definitely been on the side of the devils.

A few days later I met Franco again at the Bar Rasenna.

'*Professor*!' he called. 'Have a coffee with me.'

We drank together – the dark smear of liquid which keeps the whole country working – and reminisced like old comrades-in-arms.

'Maybe there'll be another opportunity,' he said. I thanked him profoundly but hinted that perhaps my tomb-robbing days were over. Maybe I didn't hint strongly enough.

'And that fellow, Deekes?' he asked. 'Maybe he'd like to come too.'

'Dickensa,' I corrected him. 'I don't think he'll be coming.'

The secular and the religious are delicately poised in Avea, poised both politically and socially like two masses on either end of a balance. The beam tilts and sways but never tumbles into instability.

There is of course the church. Crouched in a corner beside the rotting Palazzo Orsini, it has the appearance of a child tucked beneath the skirts of its mother. Until recently this metaphor was accurate: the church was a mere instrument of the secular arm of village life, a means by which the *signori* bolstered their rule. Now its physical position belies its importance. You only have to see the ruin of the Palace with its barricaded main door and the KEEP OUT sign to understand that. Metaphorically, at least, the church has emerged from the skirts of its mother. Don Anastasio is a power in his own right and the church of San Lorenzo, with its grey columns and shadowy corners and chapel to the Madonna, is the seat of his power.

'*Mortacci suoi*,' Grazia says when his name is mentioned. She is damning his ancestors, but it is just her habit to damn priests and her words have little force behind them. Certainly this particular priest is not deserving of her wrath for Don Anastasio is a gentle and good man. Clichés abound in Italy, but he is none of the clichés available for village priest. He is neither blind reactionary, nor cynical supporter of Democrazia Cristiana, nor mindless religious ignoramus, nor a latter-day Don Camillo. He is a pastor of souls, an ageing man (most priests are ageing: vocations are low) with a tired smile and a gentle voice. I suppose that any man of sensitivity who is constrained to sit in the fusty darkness of the confessional and listen to his parishioners' confessions is bound to acquire a tired smile. The repeated follies of modern man cannot make very inspired hearing.

Don Anastasio is also a man of some learning. Quite why he should be charged with the five thousand souls of a forgotten village rather than being called on to exercise his ability in a seminary or a school is not clear. Often his homilies, didactic but intriguing, float above the heads of many in the congregation. What, for example, could they make of his dissertation on the function of the Sanhedrin in the life of Palestine Jewry of the first century AD? Or his careful tiptoeing through the doctrine of justification as expounded by that dangerous theologian Saint Paul? But he is a good man and his parishioners recognise goodness.

'*Un bravo*', is the general view, even amongst those, and they are not few, who have espoused the other principal creed of the village – communism. Only Grazia seems to bear him ill.

Don Anastasio is also a child of the Second Vatican Council (although he was ordained into the Tridentine Church) and he is fastidious about avoiding politics in church. 'You must vote as your conscience dictates,' he urges the congregation when the elections approach. 'If you pray and you believe, then your conscience will not let you go wrong.'

There are some who might even see in that a tacit advocacy of the Christian Democrats – after all, the exhortation implies that it is *possible* to go morally astray in the election, which in turn means that at least one of the parties represented must, in Don Anastasio's eyes, be immoral. But that is probably being over-subtle about it. In nothing that he says is there anything which might give the more-or-less devout parishioner any reason to chose one party over another. No, far from being political, the priest is more outspoken on those aspects of village life which trespass on the pagan. The word pagan, *pagano*, comes from the Latin for a countryman, *paganus*. Whatever the *OED* might say, the etymology seems obvious: the early Christian religion was pre-eminently a religion of the cities; presumably pre-Christian rites, the worship of the ancient gods of the peninsula, had their longest survival in the remote countryside, far from centres of population where the new religion flourished. Thus 'countryman' became synonymous with anyone who adhered to the old ways. Don Anastasio still finds hints of the pagan and the heretical in the feasts of the church.

'We must revere the Madonna, yes,' he tells the congregation at the feast of the Immaculate Conception, 'but we must not think of her as someone who can be bribed to do us a favour with the promise of a few candles and a Hail Mary.' In the side chapel the church's treasure, an indifferent painting of the Madonna, is fenced in by wands of white wax, hedged round by glimmering little flames. 'That is how the ancient Romans used to treat their idols. But not only must the Madonna not be bribed, theologically there is nothing there to bribe. She is the mother of her Son. She is not His substitute.'

They shuffle awkwardly in the pews. Avea is a powerfully matriarchal society where the women exercise enormous, yet occult, power; and they wield it through the medium of the first-born son in a tantalising, perhaps disturbing, echo of the Marian doctrine of the Catholic Church. The good ladies of Avea are disturbed to hear a favourite doctrine questioned.

'We must, of course, honour Mary as *theotokos*, the mother of Jesus. But we must reserve our worship for her Son.'

The mothers occupying the front pews feel happier with this. Mary gave birth to the son of God, just as they have each given birth to a kind of God – their eldest sons, the ones who can do no wrong. They feel very much on the side of Mary. The Church in Italy is still suffused by the female element, influenced perhaps by the pagan world of two thousand and more years ago when the female element was given its due and goddesses vied with gods for the soul of man. The patronal saint of the church of Avea may be a male – the major and historical Roman martyr Saint Lawrence – but in the village his feast on the tenth of August vies for importance with the purely local *festa* of the Madonna del Melagrano, Our Lady of the Pomegranate Tree.

We found the sanctuary in the early days, and quite by chance, simply by walking out of the village one afternoon and up the hill past the *mulino*, the village mill. As you climb you can see back down on the village, down on to the roofscape. It is a mosaic of tilted planes, an achievement as compelling as the work of some master of abstract painting, Paul Klee perhaps. The thing is a mystery. Why should this artefact, created by nothing more than the exigencies of the building trade, acquire all the subtlety and power of a work of art? Like many such mysteries we ignored it and continued up the hill.

The road climbs up to a wooded ridge where a sign in the hedge points to BANDITA DELLA MADONNA. The words on the sign are freckled with shot marks. Beside it a track descends sharply through dense woods into the next valley. Abruptly you are detached from the village, indeed cut off from most references to modern man. There is evidence of wild boars rooting amongst the trees beside the track. Below the woods a small river meanders through water-meadows where cows graze beneath the poplars. For a moment you might be in southern England. But then you look closer at the cattle and find that they are neither Friesian nor Jersey nor any other familiar breed, but magnificent Minoan beasts with grey coats and spreading horns and the expression of creatures who have seen beyond the surface of things. They live half wild in the *macchia*, like something left over from a Bronze-Age past. It is not hard to imagine them as cultic beasts in a pagan ritual, garlanded with flowers, being led to the sacrifice.

Upstream, where the river cuts through a deep gorge, we found the sanctuary. We didn't know the story, but the sight of the bell-tower crouched in the deep V of the hills was enough. We followed the path where it crossed the river and climbed the far side of the valley. The sanctuary buildings stood on a high cliff overlooking the gorge, decaying gently in the slow passage of time: a broken wall and a gateway; ruined outbuildings of some kind; a church with a bell-tower in grey *nenfro* stone.

'I'll bet it's not open.'

'Probably abandoned.'

'Those ruins must have been a community of some kind.'

We walked across the grass and up a few steps to the entrance. The door opened on creaking hinges. There was the smell of damp inside, perhaps a faint hint of incense given out by the fabric of the building. The place was swept clean, the altar bare. On the wall of the apse, caged in iron, was a murky painting – a Madonna peering out through layers of varnish and grime into the empty space. Did we say a prayer? Perhaps we would have lit a candle had there been any available, but the small, undistinguished church offered nothing, gave nothing away.

Back outside, we poked round the ruined outhouses for a while. Directly below the buildings trees choked the gorge but beyond them the valley opened out to disclose the distant green of the water-meadows where the cattle grazed. All around us was the sound of birdsong and the seething of wind and water. High above the trees the place was a little fragment of Arcadia broken off from the past and given back to the modern world; but just as with Arcadia, something irrational lurked below the surface.

C turned towards me, wide-eyed. 'What was that?'

'What?'

'A shout. I heard someone call.'

It came again, a disembodied voice: 'Oh!'

We looked round. Another shout, echoing round the ruined buildings.

'Where did it come from?'

The sound was erratic, underpinned with jeering humour, wavering on the edge of madness.

'Eeeoh!'

'Let's go,' C suggested.

There was nothing ghostly about the place: Italy is a country haunted by the past but not by ghosts; spirits, perhaps, but not ghosts with their sly malignity, their odour of resentment and envy. One felt no dread standing there in the sunlight in the middle of the half-ruined sanctuary with a disembodied voice calling and laughing, just a small tremor of disquiet at this manifestation of the irrational.

'Maybe we ought to.'

'You're not very brave, are you?'

'You suggested it first.'

'Ha!' came the voice.

'There are windows up there,' I said, pointing to the roof of the church just below the campanile. 'They've still got glass in them.' The windows were blank, cataracted with a reflection of the sky.

'Hoh!'

I turned to say something but C was already through the broken gate and on the path.

'Wait for me!' I called. So we beat an ignominious retreat, and as we went I am certain I heard distant, triumphant laughter.

Back down in the valley we found another human, the Cowman, wandering in splendid solitude along the track, greasy hat pulled over his eyes. He carried a stick which he swung at any convenient plant that stood in his way.

'*Buon giorno*,' we said.

He glanced at us with an expression of suppressed amusement. 'For the snakes,' he said by way of explanation. 'You want to be careful of the snakes.'

'Snakes?'

'*Frustoni*,' he assured us. 'This big.' He held out both arms as a demonstration. One imagined pythons at the very least. 'They go for you, you know.'

'Are they poisonous?'

He shook his head. '*Viperi*, yes, but they're small.' This time he pointed his finger towards the ground and touched the crook of his arm. 'But the *frustoni*, they go for you. I've seen one, I've seen one chase a friend of mine. He was running and this *frustone* was keeping up with him easily. Overtaking him and rising up like this on its head' – his arm reared above his hat – 'and then – crack! on his back. And again – crack! That's why they're called *frustoni*, you see.' A *frustone* is a whip. 'I saw it,' the Cowman assured us. 'He had scars this long on his back, still has them to this day.' He paused to let the warning sink in. 'You're *gl'inglesi*, aren't you?'

We admitted as much, or at least I did. C was always careful to make her own origins clear.

'Malta? *Mai sentito nominare*.' He'd never heard of it.

'What are you doing here?' I asked. 'Apart from fighting off snakes.'

He grinned toothlessly. 'Looking for animals.'

'Animals?'

'Animals, cows.' He waved a hand. 'They come over from Vetrano and steal them. You see that stream? That's the border between the two villages. The thieves come over from Vetrano and take our cattle. Then they change the marks. *Bastardi*!'

'And what do you do about it? Do you go to the police?'

'Police?' He roared with laughter. 'What use are the police? No, you've got to beat them at their own game. They come over here and steal my cows; I go over there and steal theirs!' He grinned slyly. 'And I change the marks.' Then he lowered his voice and stepped nearer. His breath was sour. 'Problem is, I don't think anyone really knows whose cows are whose.' This anarchic idea seemed to please him enormously. He roared with laughter once again. '*Porca miseria*, we have no idea whose cows are whose!'

'What is the building up there?' I asked, when the laughter had died down.

He turned, almost as though he had never noticed it before. 'That's the sanctuary. Madonna del Melagrano. Did you hear the *matto*?'

'We heard someone shout.'

The Cowman laughed. 'He does it for fun. Harmless, really, just does it for fun. Chase you away, did he?'

We admitted as much. 'What's the story of the sanctuary? Was it a convent or something?'

'Convent? No. It's the sanctuary. The Madonna del Melagrano. You know a *melagrana*?'

'Passionflower,' C said. 'No, pomegranate.'

'A fruit,' the Cowman explained. 'Whatever you want to call it, a fruit. *Melagrana*. Well, there was this tree growing this fruit, up there above the gorge. Oh, a long time ago.' He waved his hand as though to signify the passage of centuries. And, with much ducking and weaving and many misunderstandings, he told us the story:

Many years ago (the sanctuary dates from the fifteenth century) there was a shepherd who lived much as the Cowman lives, managing his beasts on the border between Avea and Vetrano. He probably suffered from rustlers too. Anyway, one day he was up on the top of the cliff overlooking the gorge when he had a vision of the Virgin Mary. She appeared to him – 'a beautiful woman dressed in blue with stars round her head' – in the shade of a pomegranate tree that happened to be growing there.

The shepherd fell to his knees in amazement and awe. 'Wouldn't you?' asked the Cowman, and we agreed that probably we would.

'Go and tell the people of your village to come and build a shrine to me,' the Virgin Mary told the amazed shepherd. Well, of course off he went, down the track into the valley and up over the hill to Avea. Wouldn't you? And he rushed through the gate and down the old main street into the exiguous piazza in the *centro storico*, which was the main square of the village in those days.

'Hey, I've just seen the Blessed Virgin!' he shouted. 'Up on the hill overlooking the gorge.'

The old boys looked up from their cards and their carafes of cloudy wine.

'She appeared to me and blessed me and told me to tell you lot all about it,' the shepherd said.

The old boys watched him.

'We've got to go up there and build a shrine to her,' the shepherd insisted. 'She said so.'

The old boys watched, sucking their teeth.

'Well, come on, let's go!'

The old boys looked at one another. 'Pissed again,' they muttered, and went back to their cards.

The shepherd protested in vain. Then he thought of the other place, the other village, the one that shares common boundaries with Avea. Out of Avea he went, back up the hill and down into the valley, over the stream, back up to where the Madonna had appeared (she wasn't there any longer; it was entirely up to him), and down the other side. He ran the whole way, from Avea all the way to Vetrano.

'Hey, you lot!' he shouted when he finally got to the main square of the second village. 'I've just seen the Virgin Mary!' The old boys looked up from their cards and their carafes of cloudy wine. 'She appeared to me on the hill overlooking the gorge. She blessed me and told me to tell everybody about it. She said we should build a shrine to her.'

The old boys watched him. They sucked their teeth. Pissed again, they thought.

'So I went straight to Avea . . . *and they didn't believe me.*' Sober as a Calvinist, you see.

The old boys of Vetrano stirred. They looked at one another, then back to the shepherd. 'They didn't believe you?'

'Said I was drunk.'

'The people of Avea didn't believe that the Blessed Virgin had appeared to you?'

'Not a bit. So I came here.'

'We'd better see about this, hadn't we? Can't have Avea casting doubt on the Blessed Virgin. Load of bloody pagans.' And so they left their cards and their carafes of cloudy wine and followed the shepherd up to the place where the Blessed Virgin had appeared to him. And they built a shrine under the pomegranate tree. And the next day the people of Avea, feeling rather put out by the whole episode and a little worried about the prospect of crop failure, lightning strikes and the rest, came and worshipped at the shrine.

The Cowman's eyes twinkled. 'And that,' he said, 'is why, every year on the anniversary of the appearance, the people of Vetrano come here and have their *festa*; and the people of Avea have *to wait until the day after for theirs.*'

We looked round at the meadows, and the encircling woods, and the sanctuary up above the gorge. 'They have a *festa* here?'

'Oh, yes. A big *festa*. Stalls, bands, *giostre.*' *Una giostra,*

97

once a joust, now a merry-go-round. 'Makes a hell of a mess,' the Cowman said. 'The cows spend the next month eating plastic bags and suffocating.'

Apart from knowing about snakes and cows and local traditions, the Cowman was also an expert on fungi. Some days later we encountered him outside the Bar Rasenna in the village. He was sitting at a table with a basket in front of him, and in the basket was a collection of mushrooms.

'Are they good?' we asked.

He grinned slyly, as though the merit were all his. 'They are wonderful! But you must beware!' he warned us. 'There are those that are good and those that' – he drew his thumb sharply across his throat – 'those that will kill you if you touch them.'

'Show us what you've got.'

He pursed his lips thoughtfully and reached into his basket. 'There's this.' He held up a massive club-like object, white-fleshed and shaggy. '*Mazza di tamburo,*' he said. Drumstick. It was a young parasol.

'This is good. But you must beware. The most poisonous of all has white *lamelle* just like this one, and if you are not an expert . . .' He left the rest unsaid.

'How do you tell the difference?' we asked nervously.

'You *know,*' he replied enigmatically. 'You just know.'

He knew. He knew which ones you could eat and which ones you couldn't, but he also knew which you must cook before eating and which you mustn't eat if you are drinking alcohol, and which will kill you slowly and which will kill you quickly and which would send you mad and which would send you into ecstasy.

The peoples of the world may be divided up into fungophile and fungophobe. The British are fungophobe. The Italians are fungophile. It is a curious dichotomy, the kind of thing that lends itself to glib explanation, but it is nevertheless true. Come early autumn the woods around Avea are full of people

98

with baskets and sticks on the search for fungi, while the markets have their fungi stalls, and their government inspectors issuing certificates of edibility and checking any amateur's basket if asked to.

One of the mysteries – and there are many – about fungi is that the most desirable seem to resist all man's efforts at cultivation. The fact that the fabulous truffles – price far above the cost of gold – cannot be grown in captivity, so to speak, is well known. But neither can the *porcino*, the piglet, the most favoured in Italian cooking. Neither, as far as I know, can the chantarelle (*galletto*), or the horn of plenty (*cornucopia*), or the treasured Caesar's mushroom (*ovolo buono*), or the parasol which the Cowman had found. Thus the traditional search through the woods for one's own table, or the table of the nearest trattoria if you wish to make money. The cost of *porcini* and *ovolo buono* can be exorbitant. If you know a place where they appear you keep it quiet.

In the Osteria del Re in the village they produce the *porcini* with all the ceremony of Japanese drinking tea: the caps are salted and baked in the oven and make a main dish of rich and heady flavour. But the orange Caesar's mushroom, *Amanita caesarea* – named for the fact that the Roman emperors reserved it for their own tables – is so sought after as to be almost unobtainable. We found it for the first time not in a clearing amongst the oak woods which is where it grows, but in the garden of a restaurant one autumn lunch time.

A solitary customer sat at the table next to ours. He was a middle-aged man wearing rubber boots and an anorak and carrying the cane basket which is the sign of the mushroom hunter. He called to the waiter for an empty plate and pepper, salt and oil and then he picked a white bundle out of his basket. With all the care of a priest unfolding the corporal in preparation for the mass, he unfolded his little bundle. Within lay three sleek mushrooms. Their stems and gills – fine, crowded gills – were a delicate yellow. Their caps were flawless orange-red. A fourth was still enveloped in its volva. It had the appearance of a cooked egg, the yolk couched in its white.

The man noticed our glance. I suppose he couldn't help but do so. *'Magnifici, no?'*

'Marvellous,' I agreed. I had read about them, nothing more. 'Caesarea, aren't they?'

He nodded. 'We call them *ovolo buono*. But *Amanita caesarea* also. You know the story?'

'The emperors used to eat them . . .'

The waiter came over with the condiments. The man produced a knife and began to cut the mushrooms up with great care. 'The story is, as you say, that the emperors used to eat them, but also that they used to eliminate their enemies by slipping in amongst the *ovoli buoni* a specimen of the *ovolo malefico.*' He peeled the unopened one and displayed the pale yellow gills. 'You see? This is the sign that everything is all right. Otherwise it is possible to confuse them.'

*'Ovolo malefico?'* I asked.

*'Amanita muscaria.'* Blithely he sprinkled oil, pepper and salt on to the fragments of mushroom.

I guessed at the word: *'Allucinazioni.'*

'Exactly. Poisonous, if you eat enough; religious trance if you eat a little less. It must have made an interesting problem of dosage. Here, help yourself.' He passed the plate across. We protested, but he insisted we share them with him. 'It is always better to share food than to eat alone.'

And so, with a complete stranger, we sampled what is probably the most desired mushroom of all, the mushroom of the emperors, the mushroom which is first cousin to the fly agaric which was the mushroom of the druids and, probably, although the secret was never broken, the mushroom of the Eleusian mysteries. In his book *The Sacred Mushroom and the Cross* John Allegro, sometime researcher into the Dead Sea Scrolls, even suggests that Jesus Christ was merely a code word for *Amanita muscaria*. There's no accounting for taste.

# 9

While the church punctuates the life of the villager, giving it
structure and meaning – baptism, confirmation, marriage,
burial – the *comune* merely records it: birth, military service,
marriage lines, death. The council offices are a temple of
bureaucracy, a shrine to registration and certificate and
licence. In order to perform the simplest of operations – open
a bank account, undertake a hire-purchase agreement, buy a
car, get connected to the electricity or the water – you need a
*certificato di residenza*, and to ensure that you don't go around
doing all these things with an expired certificate your copy,
signed by the *sindaco* (mayor), has a life of a mere three
months. So back you come, dutifully, a supplicant at the
shrine, to get another copy. It is a mystic ritual of the great
religion of bureaucracy.

'You need to renew your *soggiorno*,' the girl behind the desk
in the *comune* informed us one day. 'I can't give you a
*residenza* if you haven't got a *soggiorno*.' I forget what it was
we were after on that occasion, but there was no doubting the
problem. Our *permesso di soggiorno* had expired: with it had
gone our right to exist.

*Permesso di soggiorno. Soggiorno*, sojourn. It has a fine
nineteenth-century ring about it, a hint of the days when
Shelley and Keats were in the city, an echo of the Grand Tour
when you travelled with letters of introduction. This evocative
document is issued not at the communal level but at the pro-
vincial level, at the Questura di Roma, the Rome central police
station. At first, in the company of Natale, we had been given
a *soggiorno* for one year.

'But we are citizens of the Common Market,' we had protested. 'Can't we have one for longer? People we know have got them for five years.'

The official shrugged, as officials will. 'They're bastards,' Natale remarked by way of consolation.

Thus, a mere year later, we were constrained to go through the agony once more, lest the *comune* of Avea strike us from the books. Experience had taught us to be up early. At eight o'clock in the morning we presented ourselves at the Questura, only to discover that the system had been changed since the previous year. Now we had to have a number.

'A number?'

'A number. Here.' The duty officer handed us a square of blue paper bearing the Questura stamp. The date and the number, 10, were scrawled in ballpoint. 'Come back on the twenty-fifth.'

'But that's in fifteen days' time.'

'That's right.'

'And if we had known we could just have phoned and booked an appointment.'

The sorrowful shake of an official head, a shake that is full of pity for those who live in ignorance of the infinite subtleties of bureaucracy. 'Oh no,' he assured us, 'you have to present yourself in person to get a ticket.'

So, fifteen days later, there we were once more, surrendering our number and sitting down to wait. 'At least it should be quite quick now,' we told each other hopefully.

The *ufficio stranieri* was a tawdry place, a jerry-built collection of offices in dull brown and faded beige that seemed to have been burrowed out of the ruins of the grand nineteenth-century palace of the Questura. There was a smell of disinfectant and sour floor-cloths. The waiting room was actually a corridor running round the inside of one of the courtyards and the cloudy windows overlooked what might well have been an exercise yard for short-term prisoners. Halfway down this corridor the floor rose three steps, then descended three more.

Presumably beneath the shoddy construction of the twentieth century lay a grand archway of the nineteenth. Officials had to clamber over the motley group of petitioners squatting there on the stairs.

We waited. The hours passed. People came and went. Bureaucrats emerged from the penetralia of the temple laden down with dusty files. No one called us.

Eventually we went over to one of the desks to ask why half the queue had passed ahead of us. 'We had number ten.'

'Your case is being dealt with. Please take a seat.'

Another hour passed. The office advertised its closure at one and the clock in the corridor now pointed to eleven o'clock. This time we demanded our constitutional rights.

'We wish to see the *capo ufficio*.'

'The *capo ufficio*?' The position might not have existed.

'Someone must be in charge here. We want to see him. We've got number ten and we've been here three hours.'

A shrug. 'Second door on the left.' Apparently there was someone in charge.

At our knock the *capo ufficio* welcomed us into her room. She gave no indication that her life hung in the balance. 'What can I do for you?' she asked politely. 'Is there some problem?'

There was some problem.

She smiled sympathetically. 'A moment, please.' She went. We sat there fuming amongst the scratched government-issue furniture and the heaps of files dating back to the *risorgimento*. She returned. 'I'm afraid the problem is that your file can't be found.'

What did that mean? Did we no longer exist? 'What,' I asked in hushed tones, 'what happens if it can't be found by closing time?' It was like waiting to hear the worst from the doctor. I barely had the courage to form the words: 'Will we have to come back tomorrow?'

'Oh no,' she replied breezily. 'If we can't find it by one o'clock we will simply open a new file for you . . .'

What would that mean? Would we then exist twice?

*

The Palazzo del Comune is also the home of Avea's political masters, the *sindaco* and the *giunta*, the mayor and council. You may, if you wish, climb creaking stairs to the second floor and slip into the exiguous public gallery of the council chamber, the *camera del consiglio*, and see democracy at work.

The council chamber is wood-panelled. It has something of the appearance of a courtroom with the *sindaco* enthroned beneath the star of the Italian republic and his councillors ranged on either side of him like magistrates on the bench. The Italian *tricolore* of red, white and green was bestowed on the Italian people by that great Italian champion of civic freedoms, Napoleone Buonaparte. The *sindaco* wears it round his ample middle and over his left shoulder as though he has been gift-wrapped; but underneath, instead of tail coat and breeches, there is nothing more than a rather crumpled grey suit. He is a member of the Christian Democrat party, but his *giunta* is, of course, a coalition.

Avea's politics are a microcosm of national politics. All factions, all fractions are here – DC, PCI, PSI, MSI, PL, PR, PSDI (and not a few others): dichee, pichee, p'see, missee, pee-elle, pee-erre, p'sdee. That is actually what an Italian newsreader sounds like when giving the political news. The voting system ensures that the choice of the people will be reflected down to single percentage points, so in Italy it is always worth founding a political party. Dichee, pichee, p'see, missee, pee-elle, pee-erre, p'sdee: incantations in a religion more arcane by far than the most obscure aspects of Roman Catholic doctrine. Add the three trades-union organisations CGIL, CSIL, UIL – cheegee'el, cheesle, wheel – and you have the whole picture. In recent times the picture has changed to the extent that the Communists (PCI) have reformed themselves and are now the Party of the Democratic Left (PDS), but the Soviet diehards have formed a splinter group called Refounded Communists (RC). Thus the numbers grow.

When the elections come to Avea the whole village is in a state of ferment, the atmosphere a cross between that of market and *festa*. People are arguing in the bars and the shops and under the trees, their fingers wagging and pointing, their hands cutting the air, rocking in doubt, praying for strength, bobbing, fingers bunched, to show incredulity, all the dumb show of Italian conversation. At the primary school the *cara-binieri* stand guard with sub-machine-guns at the ready and every so often one of the arguers will break off and stroll down the road to the school to vote, as though confession is complete and penance is done and he can now take communion.

The school children are delighted, of course – they get an unexpected holiday – and their elders turn out in huge numbers: some 85–90 per cent of the total enfranchised. Voting is not compulsory in Italy but it is compulsive; and this in a country where the political class is despised. The truth is that although politicians in Italy are, by and large, despicable, they are also distributors of patronage. There is a complex, occult mechanism of obligation and client status, *clientismo*, which operates within the village and within the country. Everyone has a stake in it. Ironically, votes matter.

The church has its feasts, so the major parties have their feasts. *Festa del' Unità*, *Festa del' Amicizia*, *Festa del Avanti*; feasts of the Communists, the Christian Democrats, the Socialists.

Shortly after we first arrived in Avea the Communist *festa* was held. In the morning we had seen preparations going on – the erection of a stage in front of the *comune*, lighting gantries going up, loudspeakers being hung, all that kind of thing – and when we returned to the village in the evening the *festa* was underway. Outside the gate the bar was working to capacity. Giuseppina was doing fine trade in *porchetta* and Oreste was selling his dried nuts. There was a bar run by party activists with a barbecue grilling sausages, and wine for free. There were stalls selling trinkets, there was candyfloss and shooting galleries and a merry-go-round, there was all the fun of the fair.

We pushed through the crowds, nodding and smiling at faces we recognised. The Cowman was at the bar brandishing a glass of red wine.

'*Sangue di serpe!*' he exclaimed. Snake's blood.

'*Frustone?*' I asked, but he shook his head.

'Vipers! *Comunisti!*' He roared with laughter.

We had a glass with him and then went on through the main gate and into the Piazza del Comune.

It was like stepping back into the October revolution. A blaze of lights carved the whole place into light and dark, into black and red. All round us banners hung in the hot night, like so many blood-soaked bandages hung out of windows as evidence of massacre. Wherever you looked there was the sly gleam of gold – that cabbalistic symbol of international revolution, the hammer and sickle. From a battery of loudspeakers the Internationale blared out on the expectant crowd.

The faithful watched the stage with all the concentration of their fellow-villagers watching the altar. I noticed one or two familiar faces – the pharmacist, someone who worked in the bank, a friend of Pippo's we had met. When the music came to a halt and a speaker stepped up to the microphone they stirred as at the elevation of the Host. The speaker was, it transpired, from Via delle Botteghe Oscure, the Street of the Dark Shops in Rome where party headquarters are situated.

'Comrades!' he shouted. He was dressed '*sport*'. He wore a dark-brown jacket and slightly flared beige trousers. All was of perfect cut. His shoes gleamed in the spotlights and a shining leather bag was slung over one shoulder. His hair was beautifully styled. He was never going to lead a popular revolution.

'Comrades!' he repeated, holding up a sheet of paper. 'I bring you the warm greetings of the Central Committee of the Party.' Cheers. 'Under our illustrious chairman, *onorevole* comrade Berlinguer!' More cheers.

We pushed through the crowd into the shadows of the Via

Vittorio Emanuele, into a strange, mediaeval peace. For all the noise of the political gathering at our backs there was a sensation here that things would not change whatever words were uttered in the Piazzo del Comune, however many votes were cast in the election. Was that for better or for worse? The Italians have a name for the conservatism which infects Italian public life. It is *qualunquismo*, the tendency to get on with your life and not worry too much what goes on around you. It enables a nation to survive and ultimately to defeat political terrorism; but it also encourages stultifying bureaucracy and organised crime.

'The forces of reaction are on the run!' came the voice of the party man. 'They are rotten from within, propped up by the forces of foreign capital!'

Snake blood? In Giuseppe di Lampedusa's classic novel *Il Gattopardo* (*The Leopard*) there is a telling moment when Tancredi explains to his adoptive father why he must go off and join the Garibaldini in their battle to overthrow the Bourbon Kingdom of Naples.

'*Se vogliamo che tutto rimanga come è, bisogna che tutto cambi,*' he tells Don Fabrizio. If we want everything to stay as it is, it is necessary to change everything.

Italy is a country beset by such paradoxes. In just such a society Fascism was born, the creed of inertia got up as a progressive idea, the force of reaction disguised as a revolution. Janus was one of the principal Latin gods and you don't get many more paradoxical than Janus. He looked both ways, to the past and to the future, to the good and to the bad. Perhaps he also turned a blind eye.

# 10

Winter. Avea in winter is an introverted place, a community thrown back on its own resources, shuttered in by wind and rain, touched by the breath of snow. On clear days, from the high ground above the village you can see the Sabine hills brushed with white; beyond them, floating on the haze of distance, are the Apennine mountains. Rain glistens on the roofs of the village and wood-smoke smudges the air and in the *osteria* in the old village the fire burns all day and all night and they serve *fagioli con le coticche*, a remarkable dish designed, as is so much of *la cucina romana*, with powerful tastes in mind. We discovered the place in the early days at our hole in the rock and we treated it almost as our dining room.

Osteria del Re, the sign proclaims in a spirit of optimism. The hostelry of the King. The story – there is always a story – is that the king of Italy once visited the Orsini Palace, Pippo's old residence at the main gate, for a day's hunting. He was a great hunter, this stout and florid monarch with his absurd curled moustaches and goatee beard. After his hunting he went for a stroll down the main street of the village. Doubtless he was mightily impressed by the glittering new street sign bearing his own name – Vittorio Emanuele II – for it was he who, in company with his Prime Minister Cavour and the extraordinary Garibaldi, had recently achieved the unification of Italy. Victor Emmanuel had a great deal to be proud of. As the eponymous king strolled down the street he expressed interest in seeing inside the house of one of his subjects. So the story goes.

A hasty confabulation amongst the *signori* of the royal party came up with the hovel of one Tancredi Bracci, halfway down on the left-hand side, as being probably the most suitable and the royal visitation was duly undertaken. The visit was a success. Tancredi was not over-awed, the children were not over-dirty, and the royal visitor even tasted a slice or two of the Bracci family *prosciutto crudo*, salted ham. He pronounced it excellent and the worthy Tancredi a stout fellow, and thus satisfied that he had sampled the way of life of one of his peasant families the king went on with his post-prandial stroll. Tancredi promptly capitalised on his good fortune and opened the *osteria*.

So much for the story. It has a certain air of truth about it – even in the days when royals were not forever being televised having cups of tea with old-age pensioners such visits must have happened, so why not here? And Victor Emmanuel II was a keen hunter. Anyway, the Tancredi thus honoured (*la signora* Bracci must presumably take some of the credit for the ham, but no one mentions her) was *bisnonno*, great-grandfather of his present successor, Tancredi II, a thin weasel of a man who is proud to show an ancient photograph of his ancestor with black hat and collarless striped shirt, but no king. And the *osteria* is there and when you step inside so little appears to have changed that you might well fancy yourself back in the parlour of Tancredi *primo*. There are four crude wooden tables and a selection of rickety old chairs. A fire rages in the mighty fireplace. Nearby, seated round one of the tables, the family are watching television (the only certain addition since the royal visit); draped in black, Whistler's mother slumped into unconsciousness, the *nonna* sleeps in the one remotely comfortable chair. Unfortunately, and to the disappointment of the eager amateur historian, this lady is from the other side of the family; and she is stone-deaf.

Intruding on this domestic scene for the first time, we thought we had made some kind of mistake. 'Can we eat?' C asked nervously.

'*Venga, venga,*' Tancredi called. His eyes never left the dazzling television. There was some variety show on the air (there is always a variety show on the air) and amongst the dull brown shadows of the room the screen provided an irresistible focus of colour and movement.

Tancredi picked up a wide roll of white paper. '*Prego, signori.*' With a royal flourish he unravelled the paper and swept it across the nearest table, then tore it expertly from the roll. '*Ecco!*' His eyes had never left the television where Domenico Modugno was just breaking into '*Volare*' for, as the Italians put it, the *ennesima volta* – the nth time.

'And what can we get for you?'

'What is there?'

'Whatever you like.'

Italians are profound optimists. In a paradoxical way it is the other side of their profound fatalism. It is the reason why if you stop a countryman to ask him the way you will always get an answer even if he hasn't the slightest idea. After all he just *might* be right, and how wonderfully happy everyone will be if he is.

'But what *is* there?'

*Volare*! – from the television – *O, o! Cantare! O, o, o*!

In reality there is not much. What there is *not* would fill a few dozen recipe books. There is, to be precise, *spaghetti alla carbonara*. *Spaghetti* (stringlets) is a plural noun: there *are* spaghetti. If *spaghetti alla carbonara* are not satisfactory then there are *spaghetti con sugo di pomodoro*, and at a push, *spaghetti con olio, aglio e peperoncino* (oil, garlic and chilli pepper). As a main course there is *pollo* or *bistecca*; with spinach or green salad.

'Whatever you like . . .'

– *nel blu, dipinto di blu*, sang Modugno, *felice di stare lassù* –

'There are also,' Tancredi added cautiously, '*fagioli con le cotiche*. It is a very *characteristic* dish.'

All this is not to denigrate *spaghetti alla carbonara* and the others. You may rest assured that *spaghetti alla carbonara*, properly cooked – with *guanciale* (pork cheek) and egg yolks (rather than scrambled eggs you must make a yellow cream sauce) and the pasta correctly *al dente* – is a wonderful, simple dish, a centrepiece of *la cucina romana*. But you find it everywhere. However, *fagioli con le cotiche* . . .

'Bean soup with *le cotiche*,' he explained.

'*Le cotiche*? What are they?'

He shrugged. 'Just pieces of *cotica*.'

'Yes, but . . . ?'

'You know. Ordinary *cotiche*.'

'I think we ought to try them.'

And so we did. And so, being of stout mind and stomach and loathing modern dietary fashion, we did time and again. And slowly the *famiglia* Bracci – weasel-like Tancredi and his beaming wife, indolent son, two little daughters and ancient, decaying *nonna* – became a part of our own life. *Fagioli con le cotiche*? Beans in a thick tomato sauce with lumps of boiled pigskin.

In winter, flocks of sheep come down from the Apennines to spend the cold months in the pastures round Avea. The shepherds live a life that is out of joint with the rest of the village, out of joint with the whole world, harking back not to classical Rome, not to the Etruscans, but to neolithic times. Occasionally

you see them in the village, in sheepskin jackets and leather boots, clumping round the place as though lost; at Christmas they wander the streets of Rome like refugees from another age, playing the *zampogna*, the Apennine bagpipes, to earn a few lire. The repertoire these days is limited to Italy's single Christmas carol, '*Tu scendi dalle stelle*', a tune about as inspiring as 'Away in a Manger', and hearing it one might be forgiven for thinking these strange figures no more than another aspect of a commercial Christmas, like so many tawdry Father Christmases . . . until you have heard them playing in the Apennine villages during the spring and summer months, playing the *organetto*, a local form of accordion, driving out the rhythms of the *saltarello*. Then, suddenly, you hear the vivid sounds of the peninsula's past, for the shepherds whom so few regard are followers of an ancient calling, one that goes back further in time than almost any other way of life . . .

Avea and villages like it are at one end of the old transhumance routes. Each May huge flocks would herd up from the Roman Campagna through the Sabine hills towards the high pastures of the Abruzzi; each September, as the temperature dropped and the first rains came, the epic journey would be repeated in reverse. Excavation of sites along these routes, resting-places which were in use up to modern times, has revealed that the same paths were being followed for exactly the same purpose in neolithic times.

As late as the immediate post-war years the journey was still being made on foot. Now, of course, we are in the era of cheap travel and the sheep go to the Abruzzi packed like tourists in three-decker trucks, but if the means of transport has changed little else has. In the mountains the shepherds still live in almost neolithic conditions, in huts – *stazzi* – which are no more than dry-stone shelters built against the hillsides. They are roofed with brushwood; the interiors are heavy with the smell of sheep cheese. On the high pastures above the *stazzi*, the flocks still graze like lice on the side of a huge, dormant animal, while the dogs – white Abruzzi shepherds – still snarl and grumble round their flanks. The dogs are not there to herd the sheep but to guard them. Even now the Apennine wolf is still perceived as a threat.

'Wolves? Wolves sometimes,' one shepherd told me as we stood on the flank of a mountain a thousand metres above the mountain town of Amatrice. 'But dogs are worse. Dogs gone wild. They get a taste, you know, and they're not afraid.' His skin was polished to a fine mahogany by the sun. His eyes smiled from squinting against the glare. He was more realistic than many of his kind about the danger of the wolf; only recently one of his colleagues had shot one and dumped the body on the doorstep of the local *sindaco* as a protest against protection laws. 'And eagles,' he added. 'Dogs and eagles. We've got a ewe up the way that's just dropped her lambs and we'll be up all night keeping an eye on her.'

His companion grinned in the background, cut off from us by the barrier of dialect. As with their neolithic ancestors, even their food is limited to the sheep, a primitive symbiosis with the animals that wander all around them – sheep milk to drink, sheep cheese to eat, occasionally the meat to grill over a wood fire. 'But it disturbs the beasts. They can smell it.'

The sheep bicker and shove one another. The bleating

follows you wherever you go, like the crying of a thousand babies.

'A hard life,' he agreed, then addressed something in dialect to his companion. They both laughed wryly. 'And the *comune* doesn't help, always pushing up the price.'

'The price?'

'For use of the hillside. They auction the grazing every spring. We've got this mountainside as far as the stream there. Do you see?' Across the valley, across a mile of clear mountain air, water cascaded over ledges and down runnels to disappear into the forest. 'We have to pay good money for it and the price will go up next year. And what do they do for us in return?'

'What?' I knew the answer.

'*Niente.*' Nothing. 'They certainly don't make the grass grow; they don't build decent refuges for us either, they don't build roads, they don't lay on water. Over in L'Abruzzo it's different. But here? Nothing. You could break a leg and nobody would know if we didn't keep a check on each other. The others have already gone down so we're on our own up here. You break a leg or something and you're in a mess. It's no life.'

Far below, the trees were touched with the first russet of autumn. We bade them farewell and went off down the mountain, leaving the bleating of the sheep behind. The cool air buffeted us, but the sun was still hot. September in the mountains. The whole world is advanced a month here. On north-facing slopes the leaves were burning orange. Wild raspberries grew in profusion just below the tree line. In a world where the vertical dimension holds sway over the horizontal we seemed remote from Avea, and yet the two places are connected by the tenacious thread of the transhumance: the two shepherds would be moving down soon, back to the lowlands, to grazing grounds not far from Avea.

It is a hard and eccentric life, but it goes on and it won't die. Six thousand years, more or less. There aren't many occupations with a history like that. It won't die, not because of the meat (New Zealand can produce it far cheaper), nor because of the wool (Australia, New Zealand, United States, India), but because of the *pecorino*. *Pecorino* is sheep-milk cheese, firm and salt when young, hard and tart when matured, an integral part of the Italian diet. It is simply beyond compare. Thousands and thousands of Abruzzese sheep go back and forth between the Roman Campagna and the Apennine mountains season after season and with them the shepherds, living high, living crudely, living in a way that is still almost neolithic, just because of the cheese. But that was probably the reason six thousand years ago.

In the mountains there is also Fra Leo. He is a different thing altogether, a Franciscan friar who is custodian of a small sanctuary above one of the villages. If the shepherds are neolithic, Fra Leo is at least in some respects mediaeval: a lay brother just like Francis was, and as suspicious of priests as any early Franciscan might have been. He laughs at them for their politicising and their ambition and their wealth, for like the founder of his order he himself is truly poor: anything he has is yours. When we visit him we bring him offerings in kind – a bottle or two of wine, some salami, that kind of thing – but always we come away having received more than we have given, and his laughter as well, and a glass or two of his memorable *grappa* made by his family in the Veneto.

'Since coming here I have grown only richer,' he claims, despite the fact that he seems only to give. He has the perfect simplicity of a man who is close to his God; and of course he would laugh to read these words.

Fra Leo came here as an eighteen-year-old thirty years ago. In those thirty years he has built a hostel out of the ruins of an old Benedictine convent which lay behind the sanctuary. Is there something symbolic about that, the friars building on the ruins of the monks? But if it is symbolic then it is marvellously outdated by some five centuries. As any Franciscan building should be, the hostel is constructed out of materials begged or borrowed. It is a twentieth-century place every bit as primitive as the thirteenth-century convent of San Damiano near Assisi, which Francis and the brothers built for the first Poor Clares. Leo has a bedroom upstairs and a day room downstairs, just inside the door from the cloister, where he writes his little homilies to deliver to the villagers at Sunday mass. It is here the men of the village come in the evenings to play *scopa* and gossip – 'to escape their wives', Leo asserts; it is here that burns an almost magical fire whose hearth reaches far out into the room without ever allowing a breath of smoke to go anywhere but up the chimney. Leo has finally been prevailed upon to install a telephone – until then the only way to contact him quickly was to send a telegram – and someone has now given him an ancient television. The abysmal reception seems to give him a perverse pleasure, as though demonstrating that the whole thing really isn't worth all the fuss.

At the back of his sanctuary – La Madonna delle Grazie – there are thick forests with wild boar and wolves; below the sanctuary lies the valley and beyond it the great mountains where the shepherds graze their sheep in summer. But Fra Leo is there throughout the year, in the blizzards of winter as well as the heat of summer. He is an outsider himself, a *forestiere*, a man from the Veneto still with a northern edge to his accent, yet he is as completely at home here as anyone can be.

Only occasionally does the twentieth century really intrude on his life, but then it may do so with a vengeance: on one occasion, after not seeing the place for months, we found that a drilling rig had been constructed on the hill above.

'They've come to drill for oil,' he told us, shaking his head more in amusement than in anger. 'Just here at the back. Oil or gas; I don't think they know themselves.'

The rig was a grotesque intrusion on the landscape, decked out with lights like a Christmas tree, whining and screaming like a banshee throughout the night.

'You get used to it,' Leo said. 'They had to get rid of my *baita*. You know that, do you?'

'They removed it?' It seemed scarcely credible. The *baita* was a wooden hut which he had built on the hill twenty years earlier.

He smiled. 'Burned it down. It seems it was just where they wanted to drill. Of course, they built me another one, a fine thing of concrete, but it's not quite the same. I'll show you the pictures.'

He had them in a plastic wallet, like holiday snaps. Presumably they had been taken by some employee of the oil company: the hut standing there amongst the woods; the hut with smoke coming from it; the hut raging with flame; Fra Leo himself smiling at the camera with the drilling crew standing round him. It is a mercy that this intrusion of the Italian economic miracle came to nothing. After a few months, having drilled in vain, the oil men dismantled the rig and went away.

Sitting before his fire in the depths of winter Leo roars with laughter at the follies of politicians and the follies of priests, at the follies of geologists and oil companies. But the greatest laughter he reserves for himself.

'*Povera bestia*!' he describes himself. Poor beast. It seems a peculiarly Franciscan appellation.

# 11

The seasons are vivid in central Italy, the rhythm of the seasons working like a tide on the countryside. The days lighten and the burden of winter is lifted and the changes stir plant and animal fluids alike, the blood and the sap. Families appear on their doorsteps in the daytime sun, absolved, for the first time in a long while, from the drudgery of humping wood. Out in the fields they are gathering the first crops after the winter dearth – *fave*, broad beans, for eating raw with *pecorino*; *carciofi romani*, wonderfully tender globe artichokes; asparagus tied into bundles like the fasces of Roman lictors or Fascist blackshirts. This is a country where the staples are delicacies.

\*

One day C came into the flat from the village and stood in the doorway to the living room with a curious expression on her face.

'I've just been to the doctor,' she announced.

I was working at a table beside the french window, the one that led out into the void. Glancing up, I saw that expression but couldn't read it. 'What's wrong with you?'

'Nothing's wrong with me. I'm pregnant.'

'*Pregnant*?'

'Pregnant. It happens, you know.'

'But you didn't tell me.'

'That's what I'm doing now.'

'But . . .' But what? *Incinta*, I knew that now. *Incinta*. Suddenly she was a different thing, a part of nature not an observer. And so, by proxy, was I. 'What did he say?'

'The doctor?'

'Well, I hope you haven't told Pippo already.'

She laughed. 'Nothing. He said that it wasn't an illness. I got the impression it's quite common.'

That evening we went upstairs to break the news. Pippo already knew, of course. 'You can tell,' he assured me. 'You can see it in their eyes.' He kept looking at C with that smile, the one where he looked as though he was about to lick his lips. Grazia wept. From somewhere a bottle of *spumante* was produced. Pippo struggled ineffectually with the cork before Grazia took it from him and opened it expertly.

'*Salute!*' We toasted the foetus, swimming like a frog in its blister of fluid.

'*Un bel maschietto*,' Pippo said. 'You can tell by the way she walks.'

The spring comes quickly, hurrying the cold aside. By March the harsh edges of winter are blurred – April is high spring, flushed with warmth and rain and the climactic blooming of flowers. You can plot the course of the season with the blossom: almonds first, like snow on the bare trees of March, then cherries as the leaves begin to open. There are Judas trees flushed pink with shame for being the tree on which Christ's betrayer hanged himself, and blackthorn blossom like a sudden, late snowfall along the hedgerows. Butter-yellow Spanish broom comes later, and hawthorn – *biancospino* – and the heavy scents of jasmine, Etruscan honeysuckle and fragrant clematis. Some are familiar in England; nothing in England has this wild profligacy, this extravagance. Wild rose, myrtle, orange, pittosporum, the morning blue of chicory amongst the grasses, cistus like paper flags waving in the *macchia*; and the transient glory of the annuals – purple vetches, wild peas dancing in the hedgerows like mauve and indigo butterflies, the poppies like gouts of blood in the fields. It is as though Proserpine is returning to the upper world once only and all the energy of nature is being spent on a single, final flowering. The hedgerows are overburdened with it, the fields waist-high, the *macchia* clotted with blooms. We found a restaurant high in the Abruzzi where they have vases of wild orchids on every table – the kind of thing that horrifies British naturalists. But the flowers' survival is not threatened: I know fields where even walking with care you are yet constrained to trample them into the grass.

Words, of course, do it no justice. Coming after a hard winter, spring is an assault on the senses which explains much about Italy – the sensual side of a culture that embraces with equal facility the ascetic. And yet the average inhabitant of Avea is unlikely to extol the spiritual wonders of the change of season. Despite Don Anastasio's patient efforts during the homilies, the *contadino* probably doesn't even connect the rebirth of the natural world with the resurrection of Christ. He sees spring in purely functional terms, a flowering that is vital for everything else. He prays there will not be a late frost – the olives are particularly capricious, refusing to set fruit if all is not well – and he prays that the pests will be kind to his crop. But the flower has to die before the fruit can be born and the connection is there in the rhythm of the festivals for anyone who cares to make it: *carnevale*, Lent, Good Friday, Easter: a flowering, a death, a rebirth.

Amidst all this, C's pregnancy seemed wonderfully appropriate. It was as though we were taking part in these tides of nature in a way that no detached observers could. We were now part of a world that up to then had merely interested and intrigued us.

For Pippo spring means horses. There are many horses kept round Avea, and as they are no longer needed for draught they can be for one thing only – racing. He shows a sentimental regard for the beasts, visiting them often, talking to them in kinder tones by far than he uses for Grazia, stroking their muzzles and patting their flanks like the Aga Khan at Newmarket. Of course, he can no more ride than he can read and write. You don't have to do it to admire it.

'You want to come with me to the races?' he asked one day.

Of course we did. His nephew was driving the horsebox and Pippo was to follow in the Alfa. 'We'll go in our car,' I said hastily.

The convoy set off after lunch, the horses staring gloomily out of their vehicle at the passing countryside. Perhaps they knew what was in store for them. We drove for about half an hour to a stretch of unknown hillside deep in the country. A crowd had gathered, as such crowds always seem to gather, summoned by a scent on the air, a murmur in the ground, a sensation that just here, today, something *marginal* was about to happen. In one field an impromptu car park had grown up. In the paddock the crowd milled freely round horses and horseboxes. It was not Ascot. It wasn't even a local point-to-point. The atmosphere was far more that of whippet-racing on Clapham Common. Near the crowd there was an ancient set of starting gates. Beyond the gates an approximate track had been marked out, running along the flat for a while and then climbing the hill towards a clump of bushes. Somewhere up there was the finishing post. The problem would not be so much winning as stopping before both rider and horse disappeared into the undergrowth.

We parked the car and pushed through the crowd to find Pippo. He was bursting with self-importance. Suddenly he was the owner, the competitor, the man of the moment, issuing orders, abusing the sallow youth who apparently was his jockey, shouting at his nephew in the horsebox . . . and still finding time to introduce us to a succession of friends and acquaintances as '*miei stranieri*'.

'*Sono inglesi, sapete?*' The friends shook their heads in amazement. Never before had the races had foreign visitors.

'Do you bet?' I asked them. 'How do you put money on?'

They grinned at us and laid their fingers against the sides of warty noses, as though betting were a secret. I noticed lavatory rolls of bank notes being peeled and thrust into expectant hands, tickets being dealt like playing cards.

'Get the horse ready!' Pippo yelled.

'I'm getting the bloody horse ready,' came a cry from the depths of the horse box. There was a wild clumping of hoofs and a snort of anger.

'Well, get a move on!'

When the horse finally emerged it was a beast transformed. On the drive from Avea it had been as tractable as a brewer's dray. Now it reared and plunged and snorted. Smoke issued from its nostrils as though from the vents of a volcano. Its eyes were wild with terror and visions.

'What in God's name have they done to it?' I whispered to C.

The *fantino* was green with apprehension.

'Get up there,' shouted Pippo.

The youth pushed a helmet on to his head, grabbed the beast by the mane and cocked a leg for Pippo to hoist him aboard. The horse bucked and stamped in protest, scattering the crowd in all directions.

'What the devil are you doing?' Pippo yelled. '*Mortacci tuoi*, can't you ride?'

The *fantino* seemed as wild-eyed as his mount, a Phaeton hanging on to the Sun God's own horse. '*Vaffanculo,*' he shouted as the horse sped away with him.

Eventually the animal was retrieved and manoeuvred into its stall as one might manoeuvre a primed and fused bomb into a mortar. All around it caged beasts, wild-eyed like tigers in a circus, seemed set on breaking the stalls to pieces. Perhaps realising the futility of this plan, one of them splayed its fore-legs and managed to get its head under the gate. In desperation the jockey grabbed at the girders round him. The horse dropped its rump and a moment later it was off down the track, bucking and darting, leaving the jockey hanging in the air, clinging to the gate. The crowd roared its approval. There was a short pause while the fugitive was recaptured and led away in disgrace. Then an expectant silence fell.

'*Mortacci vostri,*' muttered Pippo at my side.

The starter mounted his pedestal. All eyes watched him raise his hand.

'*Mortacci vostri,*' muttered Pippo once more.

The starter dropped his hand. The gates sprang open. To a roar from the crowd eleven crazed monsters exploded from their cells. It wasn't a race, it was a contest between drug companies. They hared off down the track like eleven John Gilpins, hoofs flailing, legs beating like wings, clods of earth flying about the place. Then up the short rise at the end and into the bushes and it was all over.

'*Mortacci vostri!*' shouted Pippo.

'Who's won?'

'How should I know?'

The crowd had surged on to the track and up the hill. We followed. The horses were being retrieved from amongst the bushes. Some of the jockeys had thankfully dismounted. People were dancing round them, shouting and waving and claiming victory or defeat with apparently equal enthusiasm. Pippo's horse had, of course, come last.

\*

Grazia invited us to lunch on Easter Day. 'You need feeding up,' she explained, patting C's belly. On Easter Saturday, as on every Saturday, the ritual had begun with the making of the *pastascuitta*. We were summoned upstairs to watch. A wooden board was laid on the kitchen table and a volcano of flour was created in the middle. Grazia worked like the priestess of some bizarre pagan cult, chattering and muttering all the time, calling orders to the wretched Maddalena, extolling the virtues of delicate fingertips, calling down curses on the head of the supplier of eggs for their pallid yolks (*i rossi*, the 'reds', rather than the 'yellows'), breaking eggs into the crater of the volcano and working them into the flour with her fingers, from the crater in the rim, centrifugally, like a precision machine. The volcano metamorphosed into a football of yellow rubber.

'*Ecco!*' The ball was displayed to the admiring company as a goalkeeper might show evidence of a great save. Then it went back to the marble and slowly, slowly, with an unusual, meditative calm, she began to roll it.

There was a sudden flurry of anxiety. 'The window! The window!'

Maddalena hurried across the kitchen to close it.

'Draughts,' muttered Grazia. 'No draughts, no draughts.'

The window was closed. Pondering this curious fact (could the presence of draughts be the reason why pasta outside Italy is universally awful?), we watched the dough spread with millimetre precision into a fine yellow sheet. Then Grazia took up a knife. One flinched at the sight. The blade flashed and the pasta lay in ribbons, *fettuccini*, little slices really, soft and silken and golden enough to tie around your hair. And now the two of them, priestess and acolyte, hung the strips to dry, draping them over chair backs and table, festooning the kitchen with them.

'Just enough,' Grazia muttered, more to herself than to us. 'Just enough, just right, perfect.'

The *fettuccini* were made.

Should I explain that this egg pasta is not a better version of the standard thing that you buy dried, in packets? Egg pasta has a different softer texture which perhaps goes with certain sauces; but it is not *better*. I suspect that originally egg pasta was invented when hard wheat flour was not available for making the dry variety, the eggs being added as a necessity to bind soft flour together. The grain of hard wheat, durum wheat has a higher than normal proportion of the protein gluten, and gluten, as its name suggests, glues the starch together. There is enough gluten in durum flour to make a cohesive paste with water alone. That is what dried pasta is made of, and not only is it not inferior to egg pasta, there are many – I, for one – who far prefer its firmer texture and more neutral flavour.

But egg pasta is more easily made at home and, containing eggs, it has an air of opulence about it which has perhaps made it the Sunday tradition. On Easter Sunday it is even more so. As we came into Grazia's kitchen on Easter Sunday the yellow tresses of the stuff were piled on the table and ready to be plunged into the pan.

'*Butta la pasta!*' is the command. Fling in the pasta – into boiling, salted water, of course. The phrase has a certain metaphorical value. Things are underway and cannot now be reversed. Everything is ready. Matters are beyond mere human control, for once started the process cannot be halted or paused or recovered. Overcooked pasta is simply thrown away (or fed to an undiscriminating dog) and a new supply must be prepared. It goes without saying that the stuff must be cooked *al dente*, firm to the tooth (the texture changes as you bite through – soft outside, with a firmer core) because all this nonsense that you read about in Italian cookery books is actually true. You don't put the pasta on the boil and time it while you go messing about with other things; you stand over it and keep stirring it and at intervals you extract one scalding strand to taste so that you catch it at *exactly* the right moment . . . to the nearest five seconds, say. No, you don't throw a strand at the wall and if it sticks it's okay. There are no tricks beyond having the right pasta and an abundance of salted boiling water right from the start.

Being soft, egg pasta is cooked in a brief space of time, a mere three minutes perhaps. For dry pasta people can be waiting in the next room if they can move fast. For egg pasta they have to be sitting at table. Man waits for the pasta, the pasta does not wait for man.

Once it is done, you drain it and serve it immediately. Immediately! No, you don't run it under the cold tap, or add butter, or oil, or anything (if you need to, then you need to change your pasta or your water or your style of cooking or something). And don't make too much sauce. Pasta isn't a kind of potato substitute to be eaten with a meat dish. The pasta itself is the dish, with the sauce as a garnish. Mix the two together in a large bowl before serving.

The fact is that people outside Italy – even, for goodness' sake, the French – just don't do it properly because they try to bend the rules and the rules are really very simple. Furthermore, it's no good claiming you like it that way, for if you do you are simply *wrong*. There's no argument about it. Pasta, the basic rules of pasta anyway, is simply not a matter for argument.

That Easter Sunday Grazia ladled a vast, vivid, writhing mountain into our bowls.

'*Magna, magna,*' Pippo exhorted C. 'The *maschietto* needs strength.'

He set himself to the food as though it was he who was pregnant – as by his shape he might well have been – and in true Roman fashion he did not actually eat the pasta, he drank it. Each dripping forkful would be pushed into his mouth and simply swallowed. It is a bizarre sight for the uninitiated and not a necessary part of the pasta experience. By the end of the first course Pippo's napkin resembled something the midwife might have discarded.

After the *fettuccini* there was, of course, roast lamb. The

127

engulfing of food continued. When finally the trial was over and coffee was being prepared, Grazia made her move: 'You'll not have enough room when the baby comes,' she remarked. 'Why don't you move with us to the new *palazzo*? There's a lot more room. You can live under us like here.'

'*Favoloso*,' Pippo claimed. The arguments had obviously been prepared in advance. 'Three, four rooms, bathroom, kitchen as big as this –'

'Why not?' Grazia repeated. 'We're moving next month.'

C glanced at me in surprise. 'The rent?'

Pippo replied in the manner of a man winning a hand of *scopa*. Apparently C being pregnant and raised us high in the estimation of our landlord. 'The same rent! Drink your coffee and we'll go and have a look.'

So, after the meal Grazia was abandoned to the washing-up – 'Leave her,' said Pippo, 'she's used to it' – and we drove in the Alfa up to the new building. It was no more than half a kilometre nearer the old village but still the needle passed one hundred kilometres per hour on the way.

'*Bella macchina*!' shouted Pippo above the roar of the engine.

'Do you know what Henry Ford said?'

We howled round a farm truck. 'Who's Henry Ford?'

'Ford motor cars.'

Pippo shrugged, changing up, going for a hundred and ten, a hundred and twenty.

'Henry Ford said: "Whenever I see an Alfa Romeo I want to take off my hat."'

'Why would he do a thing like that?'

'Whenever I see your Alfa Romeo I want to jump in the ditch,' I yelled.

The car shrieked to a halt amidst the odour of singed rubber. 'What did you say?'

We climbed out unsteadily. 'It doesn't matter.'

If Pippo's first *palazzo* was half-finished the second one was half-built. It was already three storeys high but it was going higher. Breaking all planning laws, a further storey was rising on the roof in the manner of a snail building a further spiral to its shell – infinitesimally and mainly during the night. High above the street the half-completed walls stood on the roof like broken teeth. On the front of the building was a sign proclaiming, in the name of the *sindaco* and *consiglio*, that all further work on the building was suspended.

'That's nothing,' Pippo assured us. 'We can still finish the other floors. I'll show you.'

Certainly the new *palazzo* had points over the old one. The view for a start: it stood against one side of the valley directly opposite the *centro storico*. And the size: as Pippo had said, it was twice the size of our present flat. But there were other touches which were indisputable evidence of its owner. On the ground floor the door from the street was just a gaping hole.

'We'll put a door in, don't you worry.'

'Marvellous. And what about the balconies?'

'*Quanti sono belli.*' He waved his hand to extol their splendour. There were three balconies, one across the front overlooking the street, one down the side, and one at the back overlooking, from a vertiginous height, the valley and the panorama of the *centro storico*. The balconies were indeed magnificent.

'They don't have any railings.'

'Don't worry about railings. We'll have the railings ready for you.'

'And there's no front door to the flat either.'

'It'll be put in.'

'And radiators. There's no heating.'

'It'll all happen,' he assured us. 'Don't worry. This isn't like the other place, this is a marvel. Room for the *bambino*, room for the family, view, everything. *Una meraviglia.*'

We inspected the place cautiously, as though expecting the floor to cave in. From the front door a corridor ran the length of the flat to the rear. Because the building actually abutted the neighbouring block this corridor cut an entire room off from the outside: there was no window, no ventilation, no light. It was a masterstroke of bad design.

'What do we do with the black hole?' I asked.

Pippo waved his hands expansively. 'Stick the wife in there when she gets tiresome.' He used the characteristic Roman phrase – *quando ti rompe le palle,* when she breaks your balls. *Romanaccio*, the Roman dialect, is that kind of language.

'But it's a huge waste of space. There's no air and no light. It's the biggest boxroom in the world.'

'You've still got three other rooms. And look at the kitchen.'

The kitchen was indeed fine. It overlooked the street at the front and wrapped round the side of the building in the shape of an L. There would be room for a dining table as well as cooker and sink and cupboards. There would even be room for an armchair or two. It was a kitchen to live in.

'What do you think?' I asked C.

'It looks fine to me.'

'We'll have them on top of us again.'

'We've put up with it till now.'

Pippo watched us, as nervous at the sound of English as he was at the sight of the written word. There was almost – almost – something pathetic about his expression. 'What do you say?'

'We must think about it.'

A month later we watched them move out of the flat above us and into the new place. There was still no door to the street and no front door to the flat itself. For the moment they hid their lives behind a curtain hung across the doorway.

'We're not moving in,' C assured them, 'if our door isn't done.'

'*Dai*!' Come on, Pippo protested. 'Have faith.'

There were no radiators in the rooms, and no railings on the balconies either.

'*Dai*! It'll all be done in good time.'

# 12

That summer we went away for a month, to Umbria and Le Marche.

'I'll do the move for you,' Grazia had insisted before we left. She was in the flower shop, dumping masses of roses and lilies into their vases, swearing at them – '*mortacci tuoi*!' – as though it was all their fault. How anything elegant and refined could come out of that shop remained a mystery, and yet that is what happened. People walked away from FIORISTA LA PRIMULA with bouquets which would have graced a florist in Knightsbridge.

'I'll get Romano and Pippo's nephew to help. When you come back you'll find everything in place in the new flat.'

'You are very kind,' I said.

'How much will it cost?' asked C.

Grazia shrugged the sum, but not the idea, aside. '*Una stupidaggine.*' A nothing.

'But how much?'

'Aren't you looking a gift-horse in the mouth?' I whispered to her. *A caval donato non si guarda in bocca.*

'How much will it cost?' she repeated, ignoring me.

'Just the petrol. And something for the boys.'

As so often in Italy, such negotiations hedged around the issue without ever reaching it. Anglo-Saxons deal in things called facts. Italy is a country of ideas and concepts; fine, indeterminate things that you cannot put a figure to for the moment. 'Petrol and something for the boys.'

'No more than twenty thousand,' C said, and added to me, in English, 'We'll go up to thirty.' She turned back to Grazia. 'And the door still hasn't been put in. I don't want anything moved until the front door is in place.'

'Of course. A door.' Grazia laughed and shook her head, busying herself amongst the vases. She, of course, was still living her life behind the roughly hung curtain.

'I want to *see* the door before we go,' C insisted.

'I'll speak to Pippo.'

'Don't worry,' C said grimly. '*I'll* speak to him.'

A few days before we left we went up to the new *palazzo* to see the door in place.

'Magnificent!' asserted Pippo, smiling. 'Look.' He swung it back and forth, demonstrating it with all the pride of a man who has just invented the hinge.

C examined it suspiciously, as though at any moment it might shimmer and wobble and dissolve before our eyes. 'There's still no street door, and no railings on the balcony,' she reminded him. 'Nor on the stairs. And what about the heating?'

Pippo shrugged, as though the front door was surely enough. '*Pazienza*,' he said. It is a word you often hear in Italy. '*Pazienza*. You've got your door, haven't you? You'll get your railings. And your heating. Winter's a long way away. *Pazienza*.'

So, with *pazienza*, we set off for our holiday. We divided July between Gubbio and Urbino and it was a summer of discovery and contentment, the last for us on our own, a preparation for something so much more than mere married life – parenthood. It was a season focused on C's swelling belly and haunted by the improbable figure of Federigo da Montefeltro, a real *duca* this time, but every bit as unprepossessing in appearance as Pippo, Duca di Avea.

Some months earlier we had glimpsed Federigo and his wife Battista Sforza in the Uffizi Gallery, in the famous diptych by Piero della Francesca. Now, amidst the limestone hills and the twin towns of his old feudal state, we felt the spirit of the man rather than merely observed his profile – the tired eye, the broken nose, the sardonic mouth. And what an attractive man we found – ugly, warlike, god-fearing, wise, surely unimpressed by the sham and the pretentious. By trade he was a mercenary soldier – he died of malaria while on campaign – but by heart he was a good man and a great patron of the arts. His capital, Urbino, was the birthplace of Bramante and Raphael, which alone should make it something remarkable, but Federigo and his son and successor Guidobaldo made it more than that, bringing scholars and humanists to the place, patronising Piero della Francesca and Baldassare Castiglione as well as Raphael, building up one of the greatest libraries in the world; and doing more even than that, creating a whole manner of living in which art and ideas become supreme over the mundane matters of politics and power: in its mannered elegance, its pursuit of an ideal chivalry, Castiglione's book *Il Cortegiano*, a book of evening conversations in the palace of Urbino, is a monument to this realised ideal. It is the very antithesis of Machiavelli's *Il Principe*.

> And Guidobaldo, when he made
> That grammar school of courtesies
> Where wit and beauty learned their trade
> Upon Urbino's windy hill,
> Had sent no runners to and fro
> That he might learn the shepherds' will.

Thus Yeats, bemoaning the idea of popular taste as a touch-stone for the patronage of great art. But he is surely wrong in his assertion, for we have it on good authority that Federigo sent commissioners round his territory to find out who was in need of financial help and how they found life under Montefel-tro rule, while he himself walked freely in the piazza and talked impartially to rich and poor alike. Easy enough to be cynical, but most rulers of his day would not even have seen the need to put on a show of interest, and our sources from the period are unanimous in saying that it was *not* a show, that Federigo was a great and just ruler without fear or favour. We can hardly doubt that the gentle and learned Guidobaldo was any-thing less than his father in this respect, so surely they would both have known well enough what the *contadini* thought of the local boys made good under Montefeltro patronage. And would the shepherds have argued with young Raffaello San-zio's success, or the fame of the architect of Saint Peter's Basilica?

The city of Gubbio, where we spent most of the month, was one of the Montefeltro possessions, part of the duchy of Urbino. It is a perfect city, a late-Mediaeval and Renaissance masterpiece of architecture washing like a silver wave against the side of Monte Ingino. The ducal palace stands at the crest, just inside the wall and opposite the modest cathedral. When we visited it the building was in the process of restor-ation – a limbo into which many an Italian treasure falls for decades at a time – but we found it quiet and curiously wel-coming despite the scaffolding and signs saying *VIETATO L'ENTRATA*. Or is that no more than a sentimental conceit? We crept round in the stillness of a hot afternoon and found the main courtyard possessed something of the perfect pro-portions of *il Corte*, the great palace of Urbino itself; but in the Gubbio palace there were no tourists, just two workmen dozing in the shade of a pillar with the debris of their lunch beside them. They didn't waken. We found a flight of stairs and went up softly to the upper floor.

The principal rooms were bare. They had an echo of the Urbino palace but none of its life. There was a small room which might, just might, have been Guidobaldo's studio, which he had decorated in *intarsio* in the manner of his father's studio in Urbino, but how could we be sure, and who was there to ask? The panelling itself, every splinter of it, was sold to America in the last century and reassembled in the Metropolitan Museum of New York; an act of the purest kind of vandalism.

'Nothing to see,' a foreman told us when we bumped into him in a gallery. 'It's just a shell.' Of *intarsio* he knew nothing. He was too tactful to point out that we should not have been there in the first place. 'They're going to turn it into an art gallery. That's what they say.'

'Federigo da Montefeltro,' I said. 'This was one of his palaces, wasn't it? And Guidobaldo was born here.'

He shrugged. '*I signori.*' The word has a spectrum of meanings, from the modern 'gentlemen', by way of 'lord' to something that is closer to the Greek word *tyrannos*, tyrant. Whatever the foreman meant by it – and in that stronghold of communism he was probably a party member and so intended it pejoratively – Federigo was exactly the latter, a *tyrannos* in the ancient meaning of the word. The legitimised bastard of a woman of Gubbio, he had taken power by popular acclaim following the mysterious death of his half-brother and the true heir, the evil Oddantonio. Fratricide? It is thought by some that the strange painting of the *Flagellation* by Piero della Francesca, which still hangs in the palace of Urbino, alludes in some way to this event, to the possible complicity of Federigo in the death. But whatever the facts, the end result is not in dispute – by Oddantonio's death the people of the duchy lost a modern tyrant and gained an ancient one, a benevolent despot under whose rule the duchy became an examplar of that rare manifestation of the human spirit in which learning and artistic achievement and good governance rank higher than any other qualities. But, like any ancient Greek tyranny,

Federigo's rule did not last. His first wife died childless, and for all her wisdom and learning Battista, his second wife, still bore only daughters – seven of them – in eleven years of marriage.

Just below the palace is a small garden of box hedges and unspectacular flowerbeds, from where one may enjoy a magnificent view over the city and the world. It owes little or nothing to the last five hundred years. In the last months of her eighth pregnancy Battista Sforza would have seen exactly that view from the rooms of the *piano nobile* in the palace. She was as well read as her husband. Perhaps in her pregnancy, wondering whether this eighth child would be the male everyone prayed for, she pondered the fate of the Greek tyrannies.

When finally the longed-for son was born, delivered in one of those now empty and anonymous rooms of the ducal palace in Gubbio, it was a moment of unashamed joy. The flags flew, '*Te Deum*' was sung and a thanksgiving mass celebrated in the cathedral immediately across the small square from the palace. How God had smiled on the house of Montefeltro! The whole city and duchy was in *festa*. The baby was christened in the cathedral and they gave him a traditional family name, Guido, and the name of the patron saint of Gubbio, Ubaldo, to whom so many prayers had been addressed. Thus Guido Ubaldo, becoming in popular usage Guidobaldo. Battista Sforza and Federigo da Montefeltro: a plain woman married to an ugly man, the two of them giving the lie to that mediaeval conceit that the good are beautiful and the bad are ugly. But, for all their goodness and wisdom, the two of them could not guarantee anything for the future, any more than we can nowadays. There was only prayer then, and there is little more now. Their son Guidobaldo was the last of the line.

Italy is a land of absurd contrasts. You can lurch from the sublime to the ridiculous so fast that often enough they become irretrievably muddled up. That is exactly what happened with Fascism, and has happened since to democracy. Throughout the last two thousand years it has happened time and again to the Church. So why wonder at the shock of our return from Umbria to Avea? We left the Duca di Montefeltro, patron of the greatest artists in the world, for the Duca di Avea, who could neither read nor write; we exchanged the memory of the over-refined manners of Castiglione's courtier for the realities of Pippo's blasphemies; we bade farewell to Laurana's great palace of Urbino and Piero della Francesca's painting of an Ideal Town for a half-completed flat and balconies without railings.

'*Porca Madonna*,' Pippo protested. 'Don't you ever give a man a moment's peace?' He looked at me with mingled admiration and sympathy.

C was implacable. 'You said they'd be put up while we were away.'

'Soon, soon.'

'Soon,' C reminded him, 'there'll be a baby in the flat. Soon it'll be crawling.'

'Anyway,' he protested, 'you've got nothing to complain about. You're getting your electricity for nothing. Put up with no railings for a bit.'

'We don't want free electricity. We're prepared to pay for it.' She added, with implacable logic, 'Free electricity won't stop someone falling off the balcony. And why is it free? We ought to have a contract with the electricity company.'

'Contract, contract.' He laughed at the idea. 'Who wants a contract? Be thankful with what you've got.'

The mystery of the free electricity remained. Whenever he was pushed on the matter Pippo became evasive and Grazia merely obtuse. '*Boh*!' she would say, shrugging. You hear the wordless plosive everywhere. It is an epitome of Roman incomprehension. '*Che me frega*? Why should I give a damn?

'We'll pay anyway,' C decided.

'Oughtn't we to go to the company and ask about it?' I suggested.

'You wouldn't get anywhere, or if you did you'd just stir up trouble. We'll pay Pippo.'

'But he doesn't want any money.'

'He's going to take it whether he likes it or not.'

So every month she solemnly paid him our estimate of what we had consumed and thrust a handwritten receipt beneath his nose. It must have been the only time in his life that he had been reluctant to take money. He laughed nervously and scrutinised the words as though mere concentration might give him the clue to their meaning. Every month, muttering '*questi stranieri*' in a puzzled voice, he inscribed his laborious signature at the bottom of the receipt. We have them to this day, symbols of C's eccentric determination to be within the law.

But whatever we might do about electricity, for the moment it seemed that we had no choice but to put up with the lack of railings. It was high summer and, precipice or no, the windows had to be open. Besides, from the back balcony suspended high above the valley, we had that magnificent view of the *centro storico*. How could we not sit out there and watch the evening sunlight slanting on to the stones of the old village, tinting them the colour of Roman stucco, ochre and burnt umber and pink? The swifts screamed and swooped in the limpid air. The dusk gathered round like a warm cloak. The birds retreated to their nests and the bats came out to take their place, a dozen or more different species flickering in the shadows like pieces of charred paper thrown up from a bonfire, and in the stillness you could even hear the hum of conversation at the tables outside the main gate. Somehow, with that view before us, we sensed the spirit of the place itself, the whole organic being of the *paese*, its past as well as its present, its soul as well as the outward hulk of its body. Who cared that the balcony hung over the void and it had no railings and somehow the platform itself gave the illusion of sloping gently downwards as though it was trying, without being noticed, to tip us into the abyss?

So with our chairs nervously back from the brink we would

138

sit there sipping wine, witness to some kind of achievement of the human spirit, modest beside the glories of Urbino or Gubbio, but real enough to those with the sensitivity to feel it. Of course, just as we could watch, we could also be watched.

'I see your *stranieri* have moved in to the new place,' one of the cronies remarked to Pippo as they sat at a table outside the bar playing *scopa*. He nodded across the valley towards where we sat on our death-defying balcony.

'English,' Pippo replied, with a hint of pride.

'English.' The concept was considered slowly. 'Still no railings on the balconies?'

'So what?'

'Looks pretty dangerous like that, and the *signora* pregnant.'

'Dangerous! If they keep back there's no danger. They're adults, aren't they? Anyway *we* haven't got railings either. If the *padrone* doesn't have railings, why should the *inquilini*?'

'That's your affair.'

'Of course it is.'

'But if anything were to happen to the child, her being pregnant, then you'd be in trouble. Them being your tenants. Her being pregnant . . .'

'Trouble?'

'Oh, yes.' The crony nodded with great authority. 'The law would hold you to blame . . . if anything happened to the baby. A fright. Born blind. Anything.'

'The law?'

'I reckon.'

The law held nameless terrors for one who was constitutionally illegal. The next day Pippo came knocking on our door. '*I ferri*,' he announced with a triumphant smile. There is a proper Italian word for railings – *ringhiera* – but Pippo never gave the slightest hint of knowing it. For him they were always *i ferri*, the irons. Romano and friend were already lugging the things up the stairs, bashing them against the corners.

'I promised you, didn't I?' Pippo said thrusting out his chin like Mussolini. 'A man of honour, I am. A man of his word. *I ferri*, as promised.'

It was not surprising that the matter of the railings was ultimately settled by C's pregnancy, for a pregnant woman is the most powerful being in Italy. As C paraded through the village in those days she was watched by dozens of eyes, admired by every man, envied by every woman who wasn't also pregnant. Amongst a people who are always suspicious of the future a pregnant woman is a symbol of hope, a proof that the blessings of God do exist.

There was also a darker side to it. 'Try some of this,' they would insist in every shop she entered. A piece of cheese, a slice of *prosciutto crudo*, a peach, a bunch of grapes, anything her eyes might light on for a moment was thrust into her hand. Choice and selection had become impossible. She lived in a Midas-like state, having only to touch something for it to be, not gold, but hers. '*Magna, magna*,' was the cry. Eat, eat. The fear was that by suppressing some momentary fancy she might cause the baby to acquire a birthmark. The supposed cause becomes the name itself: such a mark is called *una voglia*, a craving. When Gorbachov first visited Italy one of the leading political cartoonists, Forattini, portrayed him full face over the title *La Voglia*. In the drawing Gorbachov's own birthmark on his forehead was a miniature map of the world.

The primitive and the superstitious lie close below the surface of Italian life. *La iettatura*, *la iella*, the evil eye, is a reality. Near us in Avea there lived a young woman who was thus cursed. She was a pretty girl, newly married, proud of her new baby, the kind of person whom one might consider to be blessed in life. Her husband had quite a good job – he was a travelling salesman of some kind – and all seemed well with them. But this girl, Alessia was her name, was *una iettatrice*, a possessor of the evil eye.

Grazia shivered when Alessia's name came up in conversation. 'That woman.' She made the sign of *le corna*, the horns, which is most efficacious against the evil eye. You clench your fist and extend the index finger and the little finger downwards towards the floor, but you must be careful with it because it is a powerful and ambiguous gesture: pointed upwards it changes significance and becomes the cuckold's horns, a curse so powerful that it will drive civilised men to fury. 'She came into my shop the other day,' Grazia told us in evidence of Alessia's affliction, 'to buy some flowers for someone – who'd take flowers from her? – and do you know what happened?'

We didn't.

'Within the hour all the roses had withered and someone had upset the vase of lilies all over the floor.' Of course we laughed, but Grazia was not joking. 'You keep away from her,' she advised C. 'Don't let her look you in the eye.'

*La iettatura* is not a voluntary thing in the way that being a witch is voluntary. It is more in the way of an affliction, like a club foot or a harelip. In a sense the sufferers are to be pitied, but that doesn't make them any less dangerous. Poor Alessia, slim, attractive, blessed with a charming little boy and a pleasant and loving husband, was to be shunned as the carrier of contagion is shunned.

'Have you noticed the boy?' Grazia asked us with heavy significance.

We hadn't.

'He's got a squint.' The prosecution case rested.

Perhaps it is worth mentioning that this is not mere village superstition. It runs deep and it runs wide. During our first days in Italy there was an outbreak of cholera in Naples and the President of the Republic, Giovanni Leone – I give his name just to impress upon the reader that this is *true* – visited one of the hospitals where the cholera victims were being treated. With proper use of rehydration techniques and antibiotics, epidemic cholera is, of course, completely curable. Anyway you have to ingest the cholera bacterium to catch the disease in the first place, so in all logic President Leone had nothing whatever to fear as he toured the wards, bringing official sympathy to the sufferers. However, a photographer in the party following the President managed to take a picture which made the front pages, a picture which demonstrated that more than mere human sympathy and medical science was uppermost in the President's mind. As Leone paraded down the ward with his hands clasped behind his back, the photographer spotted him making the sign of *le corna*. The President was warding off the evil eye.

So, from the villager in Avea to the President of the Republic, the weird rites of superstition still hold sway. Can one wonder that the arcane and mediaeval science of birthmark analysis still thrives in Avea, that *una voglia* remains unfulfilled only at nameless but real risk to the baby, and that the expectant mother is nurtured and coddled like a prize cow in calf?

'It's absurd,' we said, more than once, laughing the idea to scorn. 'How can something like that affect the baby? It's just superstition.'

And from behind the counter Giuseppina, proffering a slice of salami or a flake of *pecorino*, would laugh with us. 'Of course,' she agreed. '*Superstizione*. A stupidity. But better be sure.'

# 13

The feast of Saint Lawrence falls on the tenth of August. Saint Lawrence, deacon and martyr, is the patron saint of Avea and the *festa* is the summit of the year, the climax of everything anyone has dreamed of or worked for throughout the last twelve months. It is difficult to overemphasize its importance.

Unlike many a saint – Saint Christopher, for example – Lorenzo's existence and story are well attested. The event occurred in AD 258, in the reign of the Emperor Valerian, four days after Pope Sixtus II and six of the seven deacons of the Roman Church had been killed. With seven judicial murders under his belt, the prefect of the city must have been full of confidence as he summoned the sole surviving church leader to demand that he surrender the treasures of the Church. Poor, lonely Lawrence.

The manner of Lawrence's going is interesting, and naturally is the subject of much expert denial. 'Probably beheaded,' the experts say. It is a curious characteristic of historians that they always assert the least interesting possibility as the most likely, as though they live in a different world from ordinary people, a world where nothing new or bizarre ever happens. But the ordinary man knows that in the real world the bizarre is the norm. So let us for goodness' sake listen to Tancredi Bracci, the common man of Avea, on the manner of Saint Lawrence's going: 'They roasted him,' he tells us with a certain amount of relish. 'Roasted him on the gridiron. Just like in a trattoria.'

No blasphemy is intended. Lying prostrate in his agony, the saint himself made the same joke and rather less subtly –

'You can turn me over now,' he is purported to have said; 'I'm well enough done on that side.' And then later, perhaps with reference to the Eucharist itself and, one presumes, his imminent union with Christ, 'My flesh is well done now: you can eat it.'

On that distant day in Imperial Rome Lawrence was buried outside the city walls in a cemetery on the Via Tiburtina. A short time later the basilica of San Lorenzo fuori le Mura, one of the five major basilicas of Rome, was erected over his tomb. The cemetery around it has become the main burial ground of the city and Lawrence himself has become one of the favourite saints of a city which boasts more saints and more sinners than most.

Throughout the year his effigy stands in a glass case immediately inside the main door of the church in Avea. He is a fresh-faced young man, dressed in the red dalmatic of a deacon and with his gridiron by his side. He doesn't have the look of the hero about him, more the dreamer – but then that was probably also the truth. The people, particularly the old ladies, are fond of him in the way they might be fond of a grandchild, so there is always a flock of lighted candles in front of the case. The awful gridiron gleams in the flickering light. Truly it looks just like something from the Osteria del Re just down the road.

Only on his feast day does he leave the security of the church. The preparations for this exit take enormous amounts of energy and money. It is like preparing for a royal visit. The streets are swept, illuminations are hung across the roadway, a programme of entertainment is drawn up. There will be a foot-race for children, and a cycle race under the aegis of the Avea Cycle Club, and a *palio* – a horse race – which Pippo's horse will lose. There will be stalls selling sweets and candyfloss, there will be dodgem cars and roundabouts and a shooting range. There will also be a concert given by the village band and a display by the *gruppo folkloristico*. This hybrid term is as painful in reality as it appears on the page.

144

Folklore is not a concept which means very much in Italy. To the people of Avea the village *festa* is not folklore – it is simply what happens on the feast of Saint Lawrence. There has always been a *festa* and there always will be a *festa*. Folklore, that manifestation of northern European self-consciousness, that cosy, mythic revival of things as they never were, is quite foreign to the unsentimental Italian mind. If a thing is worthwhile – if it is good entertainment, or of religious significance, or a fair way of making a bit of money (and the *festa* is all three), then it will survive. If it is none of these things, then why waste tears over it? Folklore group? Avea's *gruppo folkloristico* is pure farce, unabashed bad taste, perfect kitsch. It is nothing more than an ill-trained gaggle of drum majorettes, complete with batons and pompoms and sickly, beauty-queen smiles.

There they are in the early evening of Saturday, parading in flounced skirts and shakoes before the village band. The tassels wave and the batons twirl. The mothers wipe tears from their eyes and the people look on admiringly and the band goes *parp!* – a sound of the most impressive flatulence modified by a wail of clarinet and a rattling of drums. It is a musical strain interpreted literally. Later on the *gruppo folkloristico* calms down for a while and allows the band to break into a familiar tune which has been Italy's unofficial national anthem since the days of the '*Risorgimento*', the Jews' chorus from Nabucco. Rarely has it sounded more lugubrious.

But the great attraction of the Saturday will come at the end of the evening. For weeks posters have announced it from every wall in the village: an open-air concert outside the main gate in Piazza Garibaldi given by one of the stars of Italian popular music, Little Tony. Little Tony is an Elvis Presley look-alike who came to stardom in the early sixties. His act has remained unchanged in a quarter of a century. He is a drum majorette of music.

A stage has been erected for him outside the main gate and all afternoon a team of technicians are at work with amplifiers and loudspeakers and cables and microphones. The sound of *'Provo, uno due tre quattro cinque'* is loud in the land. A gaggle of old men, deprived for a moment of their peace and their accustomed table under the holm oak, watch dispassionately. A young man wearing cowboy boots fiddles expertly with a mixing unit. The sound of the village band, performing inside the gate, does not intrude on the arcane preparations for the erstwhile king of Italian pop music.

As the hour approaches and darkness falls, an audience – the whole of the *paese* – materialises under the trees. Expectancy rises. Little children run and shriek around their parents' feet while their older brothers and sisters, reared on tougher stuff than Little Tony, affect a blasé detachment about the whole thing. But everyone watches expectantly as the backing group climbs on to the stage and takes up position. There is a scattering of applause. One of the group slings his guitar, flicks a switch and fires a chord off into the night. There is a howl of feedback and a hasty adjustment of some errant control before things are just right. The drummer pulls his battery into position, then plays a riff and hits a cymbal in an exploratory manner while the keyboard player begins a boogie-woogie. The crowd thickens.

*'Signore e signori,'* a voice calls over the public-address system. Its owner is an insignificant figure in the shadows, a mere acolyte at the altar. *'Signore e signori, attenzione prego.'*

To one side, away from anyone's attention but noticed by almost the whole crowd because this is an Italian crowd and it misses nothing, a white limousine has drawn up in the shadows opposite the bank. A white figure climbs out amidst a pack of dark attendants. The keyboard player begins to play a familiar sequence of notes, soft at first, then rising. C-G-C.

*'Signore e signori, vi presentiamo . . .* Little Tony!'

The drums pound. The music crescendoes in great bursts of amplified sound. C-G-C. It is, of course, the theme from *2001, A Space Odyssey*, although Richard Strauss might have recognised it under a different title. At the very moment that the World-Riddle Theme from *Also Sprach Zarathustra* sprays into its climax, the glittering, diminutive figure runs from the shadows and bounces into the lights. Applause breaks out, the whole village cheering and clapping, Avea paying homage to one of the gods of kitsch.

'You ain't nuttin' but a Houn' Dawg,' Little Tony accuses the packed crowd, 'a rockin' all de time!' His figure shines in the spotlights. The hips writhe. 'Ahwell youain'evercaughta-woman an' youain'nofren'amine!'

Recognising a fellow being, the drum majorettes in the front row of the audience scream and weep and call for more. Little Tony obliges. 'All Shook Up', 'Blue Suede Shoes', 'Are You Lonesome Tonight', the voice wobbles erratically through them all, slurring one word into another until any meaning they may once have possessed is quite lost. Even after all these years the transatlantic accent is flawed, but the people of Avea don't know and couldn't care. They are happy, for this is a manifestation of that place which they can occupy only in their imaginations or by moving away from the village – the outside world.

'*Grazie, grazie. Siete favolosi, favolosi.*' The mindless hyperbole of the sixties translates exactly: 'You're fabulous, fabulous.' Stooping, he holds out a hand to the fans in the front row while they howl and wail. Then he straightens up and continues, oblivious to the sweat on his brow and the hot summer night, oblivious to all but the cry of the crowd and the facile music. Truly he is a trouper.

> 'Is now or never, come hole me tie,
> kissme my darling, be mine to-nie.'

The applause rises both in volume and pitch. This is part of the myth which Italians can claim for their own and for the finale, straining his voice to its not very considerable limits, Little Tony even slips into the original language, going falsetto at the last:

> '*O sole mio, sta 'nfront a me!*'

Roars of applause mingled with the baying of electric guitars and the pulsing of the drums. The sound booms round the village and reaches up into the heavens with ease, telling Saint Lawrence that all is just the same with the world and the pagans are still around.

But Sunday is, of course, the true climax of the *festa*. It is important not to muddle the two parts, the sacred and the profane. Perhaps all these village feasts have their origins in pre-Christian times and maybe that gives a certain justification to the profanity of the Saturday evening. But Sunday, while no less festive, is different. Little Tony has already been forgotten. On Sunday, beginning at eight o'clock in the evening, there is the procession of the saint.

'Who, living in the twentieth century, can doubt the truth of the story?' Don Anastasio asks of his congregation. He smiles on them, the smile of a man who, though no more than a village priest, has understood a great deal in the course of his life. Packed between the grey pillars of the church, the whole village seems to be waiting for the familiar and comforting story. Only Renzo, the bearer of the processional cross, is taking no notice. He is the village simpleton, who has always held the processional cross and perceives the arrival of a new deacon, who would also like to bear the cross, as a real threat. At the moment he stands to one side and mutters urgently at one of the grey columns, as though it is the deacon himself that he sees before him.

'It is all too familiar to us,' the priest insists. 'Saint Lawrence is the missionary in Mozambique facing the guerrillas. He is the bishop in San Salvador dying in his church. He is Father Maximilian Kolbe murdered in Auschwitz.' There is a finely timed pause. 'But he is also the Palestine Arab facing up to the army of occupation, and the rabbi in the ghetto defending his synagogue against the Fascists and the Nazis.'

The shadowy church gives a small, collective shudder at the thought. The congregation stirs uncomfortably, wanting only

148

pious stories of acquiescent martyrdom and visions of glory, the familiar story that has been related time and again. Their minds are decorated with holy pictures. But now Saint Lawrence, the plaster statue on the trestles at the back of the nave, lives. And he is a difficult and disturbing hero.

The priest holds out his hands helplessly. 'The church was not rich. It was a pilgrim church, a church of the poor. In those days there was no Banco Ambrosiano.' At the mention of a financial scandal that threatens to envelop the present Church of Rome there is some nervous laughter. People mutter amongst themselves, looking round to see if all this is quite right. Don Anastasio is tiptoeing across very dangerous ground indeed. In the front row of the congregation sits the *sindaco*, wearing his tricolour sash. Beside him is the Captain of Carabinieri, silver gleaming on his black uniform. Their faces are impassive.

'So Lawrence assembled the only treasure he knew of, the poor of the city, and he brought them before the prefect and presented them to him. "These are the treasures of the Church," he said. "They are all we have."' The priest looks at them, every one of them from front row to back, with that familiar, tired smile. 'The poor of the city are still the treasure of the Church,' he tells us. 'Not the money in the bank, but the poor and the destitute on the streets. Those are still the treasures of the Church. So it was then, so it is now. Blessed are the poor in spirit, for they shall inherit the kingdom of God. And so it was that Lawrence followed his companions in glorious martyrdom, and on that day, one thousand seven hundred years ago, he was united with them in Christ.'

The congregation relaxes. This is more like the story they know.

The priest seems to be thinking aloud. 'But would the same thing still happen today?' he wonders, and gives no answer.

Mass on the evening of the *festa* takes a long time. While the stout members of the Confraternità di San Lorenzo stand guard beside the statue, almost the whole congregation shuffles up to take communion. People push in from the piazza outside, where the mass has been relayed by tinny loudspeaker. The shifting streams of people move against each other and jam themselves in the narrow space of the church.

Finally it is finished. The last Host has been dispensed to the last communicant and the monstrance is hoisted on high above the people. Acolytes hold a canopy over it and the deacon merely carries a pole with a loudspeaker at the top. In golden chasuble Don Anastasio moves off down the nave in the wake of the processional cross. For, on the feast of his namesake, Renzo the simpleton knows exactly what to do. He reaches the main door and there he pauses. The saint stands to one side encircled by the men of the Confraternità robed like the Ku-Klux-Klan but with the gridiron embroidered on their left breasts. They crouch beneath the lifting-poles. Faces glisten in the candlelight as they take the strain. On a muttered word of command they straighten. Swaying in the candlelight, the saint ascends towards the ceiling, his face wearing that expression of faint surprise.

The congregation mutters approval, as though each step in the procedure is part of a complex ritual which must be done just so, lest untold disaster befall. The crowd at the door parts like the Red Sea before the Children of Israel and Renzo marches out. After him comes the members of the Confraternità, then the statue itself, then Don Arcangelo with the monstrance and the deacon with the loudspeaker, then the *sindaco* and the Captain of Carabinieri, then the doctor and the lawyer and the pharmacist and the bank manager, and then the whole congregation in solemn procession.

Out in the piazza the crowd erupts into applause as the statue emerges. '*Viva San Lorenzo!*' they cry. '*Evviva! Evviva!*'

The statue pauses on the steps and gazes around with an expression of bewilderment. The drum majorettes are there in solemn ranks beside the band in their blue-and-grey uniforms. As the bandmaster raises his baton and the band begins to blast a solemn march into the air, the drum majorettes shamble forward. The saint teeters down the steps into the piazza. San Lorenzo is out on his annual circuit of Avea.

The object is, presumably, twofold. Partly it is to show the statue to all the *paese*, but partly it is to show the *paese* to the statue. The former is, one imagines, at least arguably orthodox; the latter is, surely, purely pagan. Nevertheless San Lorenzo obliges. He is a benevolent lord of the village, a courteous patron. Bathed in ethereal light (there are some lamps rigged up on his base), he parades through the tortuous alleys of the *centro storico*, nodding and swaying to the people who hang out of windows to wave at him, pausing every now and again to give the priest an opportunity to intone Hail Marys through the loudspeaker. Below him the members of the Confraternità perspire and groan. They are in a different world from the saintly one on high, an infernal world of sweat and labour. When the prayers come the bearers sigh with relief, for this is when poles are shoved beneath the statue to take the strain, allowing them to rest for a moment. Some of them even have a quick smoke in the shadows. In the world of light above them San Lorenzo barely notices. His golden halo shines. His crimson dalmatic is ablaze with gold thread. Lights leap and flash from the gridiron. As he died by fire so he now seems to live by fire: a towering, flickering pentecostal flame swaying in the air between the close buildings of Avea.

The procession lasts for hours. You can join for a while and then break off to have a drink in the bar or wander round the stalls of candyfloss and *torrone*, nougat. But even if the saint is out of sight for the moment, the whole village seems alive to his presence out amongst the people. There is something in the air, a vibrancy, an energy like the sensation of electricity in the atmosphere before a summer storm. Truly Saint Lawrence lives.

'È bravo,' Tancredi asserted when we encountered him in the bar. His tone suggested that the saint was known personally to him and was a common-sensical sort of man, the kind that you could rely on. 'Of course, he means a lot to me and my wife, he being the patron of cooks . . .'

'The what . . . ?'

He shrugged. 'The patron of cooks. They cooked him, didn't they? *Alla griglia*. And he knew just when he was done.'

'But is that . . . official?'

'Of course it's official.'

'Isn't it a bit' – I struggled for the word – '*morbido*?'

'*Morbido*?' Tancredi considered the possibility seriously for a moment, as though I was party to some inside knowledge. 'Not *morbido*,' he said decisively. '*Ben cotto*.' Well cooked.

'You mean *morboso*,' C whispered. '*Morbido* is soft.'

I meant *morboso*. '*Morboso*,' I corrected myself, '*morboso*. To make him patron saint of cooks, I mean.'

'Ah, *morboso*. And why is it *morboso*? Isn't Santa Apollonia the *patrona* of dentists?'

'Is she?'

'She had her teeth torn out. And Santa Lucia is the patron of oculists.'

I blenched. 'Her eyes?'

'You know the story?'

'Eyes on a plate. I've seen paintings.'

'When a pagan tried to court her because of her beautiful eyes, she tore them out and handed them to him. "Now leave me alone for God," she told him.' It seemed that Tancredi was an expert in morbid hagiography.

'All rubbish,' said a voice behind him. 'Saints and relics and everything. Pure superstition.'

The diminutive Tancredi turned and found himself looking up at the pharmacist, an imposing bull of a man who was prominent in the local communist party. 'All this,' he said, waving his hand towards the stalls beyond the windows of the bar and the effigy of the saint somewhere out in the streets of the village. 'All this is just the opium of the people. Don't give me saints,' he said.

Tancredi glanced at him without rancour. The little man

was not going to give an inch to the big. 'And what about you lot?' he asked. 'What the hell is Lenin, if not a relic?'

Once the procession has threaded the alleys of the *centro storico* down as far as the Colasanti house at the end, it winds its way back towards the main gate. We emerged from the bar to watch it pass, the drum majorettes still at the head, Renzo still leading the statue with the processional cross held aloft. The procession paused in the gateway so that the customers of the Bar Rasenna could benefit from a decade of Hail Marys.

'*Santa Maria, piena di grazia, il Signore e con te,*' the habitués of the bar murmured along with the Confraternità di San Lorenzo. 'Blessed art thou among women and blessed is the fruit of thy womb, Jesus.'

Even the pharmacist stood silent for a moment. Then the band struck up and the procession moved on towards the new part of the village. There was something faintly incongruous about its presence there amongst the concrete-framed apartment buildings, but San Lorenzo is well capable of overcoming such anachronisms. He is, as Don Arcangelo had already told us that evening, a saint for all seasons and all places, a martyr who is killed today no less than he was killed one thousand seven hundred years ago in Imperial Rome. Somehow his presence in the streets of Avea seems to unravel the warp and weft of history and show it all for what it is, the plain experience of mankind, a constancy throughout the ages. The pharmacist's objections appeared paltry.

Not until near midnight does the effigy return to its church. The Piazza del Comune is packed to see it. The people are still shouting: '*Evviva San Lorenzo!*'

It is a moment of high emotion. Riding high and unsteadily above the throng, the saint appears to have drawn a tight circle of fascination around himself. The band, tired after their marathon, are still spraying brassy notes into the night sky. Like spent swimmers, the bearers finally struggle to the church steps. They turn the statue to face the crowd and the people applaud the sight, the last sight of the *patrono* for a year, and he looks back at them in bemusement, as well he might. There is a final benediction and then the effigy rocks and tilts and goes up the steps into the shadows. The cheering and clapping doubles – '*Evviva San Lorenzo!*' and a detonation in the night sky announces the first of the fireworks. Hurriedly we make our way out to the Piazza Garibaldi to witness the display, the gold and silver showering overhead, the great concussions of the petards. Fiery rain cascades above us, fountains of golden light, blossoms of flame and colour, great circles opening up in the night sky like ripples in a black pond. The people gasp and sigh, overwhelmed by the tiredness and the excitement.

There is another thing about the night of Saint Lawrence: even after the fireworks are over and the crowd has drifted home, if you look up into the sky you will often see hairlines of gold laid across the blackness, a score or more of *stelle cadenti*, shooting stars. '*Le lacrime di San Lorenzo,*' we were told. The tears of Saint Lawrence. The astronomer will explain that at that time of the year the earth passes through a cluster of asteroids and the effect is purely astronomical, but of course no one believes that. Every night on the feast of Saint Lawrence the saint truly weeps.

# 14

Autumn, the season of fruits, the season of fungi. C was great with child and approaching her time and people fussed and clucked around her and pronounced the baby male from the way she was carrying it, and offered a plethora of contradictory advice about what to do before, during and after the birth. Where was C going for the great event? they all wondered. We would name the nearest public hospital, and then watch the ensuing conflict between politeness and misgiving in their expressions. Everyone in Italy has his favourite hospital horror story and once the politeness had been overcome we heard them all.

'Two years ago they had salmonella in the maternity wing and all the babies died.'

'They got my cousin's baby muddled up with someone else's.'

'When my nephew was in there they had to amputate someone's leg, but they cut the wrong one off.'

'When my uncle was there they didn't just get the leg wrong, they got the whole person wrong – cut the leg off a man who was in for kidney stones.'

Pia recommended some expensive private clinic in Rome as the ideal place to bring one's young into the world, a place where you wallowed in your own miniature swimming pool while giving birth. 'No pain at all, *cara*. Just a sensation of floating, of peace. And no trauma for the baby. The baby grows in water,' she explained usefully, 'and so it's only natural that it should be born in water. That way it will grow into a gentle and contented child.'

Which has no more foundation in logic than insisting that the child also be reared in a swimming pool. And it was, of course, impossible to point out that her own younger son, delivered in this manner, was a spoilt and aggressive brat.

'Let me get in touch with my gynaecologist for you,' she insisted. In vain did C explain that she was quite happy with the doctor she had been seeing at the hospital. '*Cara*, listen to me and believe me. You can't *trust* the state hospitals. They are butchers. They are filthy. I'll ring Doctor Bianchi for you.'

'The one I've been seeing at the hospital is called Bianchi.'

Pia shrugged her elegantly built-up shoulders. 'It's a common name. But *my* Doctor Bianchi is *not* a common gynaecologist . . .'

'And anyway we couldn't afford your clinic.'

'We can deal with that afterwards.'

We couldn't dissuade her. She rang her clinic with the swimming pools and asked for the revered Doctor Bianchi. He wasn't there that day. It transpired that he only worked part-time at the clinic: the remainder of the time he spent in the public hospital. The Bianchi of the clinic and the Bianchi of the hospital were one and the same man.

'So why should I go to the clinic where I would have to pay?' C asked triumphantly.

Pia was not to be put off. 'There are no swimming pools at the hospital,' she asserted. This was undeniable.

Against Pia's experience there was that of Oreste's wife. One evening when we went round to see them, she ushered us up the exiguous staircase to demonstrate the very place where she had given birth to Giuseppina.

It was all very different from clinical swimming pools. The bed lay in the shadows of their tiny bedroom like an altar to a forgotten god. On the wall above hung an oversize rosary encircling a painting of the Sacred Heart of Jesus. The window was tiny, the smell of damp powerful.

'On this very bed,' Lucia announced with a fine sense of the dramatic, 'I lay and suffered.'

Considering the size of Giuseppina, suffering was only to be expected. Indeed, seeing her at the salami counter of the *alimentari*, it was difficult to associate Giuseppina with the process of birth at all. One rather imagined a kind of special creation, an emergence in full glory from the bowels not of Oreste's ancient wife but of the earth itself.

'There was just the *levatrice* to help,' the old lady told us, adding darkly and glancing over her shoulder lest the long-dead midwife might hear, 'and blind drunk she was too, blind

157

drunk. She'd seen too many monsters in her time, that's what they said, too many monsters.' The old lady laughed and shook her head. 'Lots of monsters in those days. We didn't have hospitals and doctors and things like now, you see. There was just the *levatrice* if you were lucky, and your mother, and the Madonna del Parto.'

I noticed Oreste making the sign of *le corna*. Her tale bewildered me. Was it the hospitals which now prevented the monsters or – it seemed unlikely in this Godless age – were the prayers to Our Lady of Childbirth more efficacious these days? Or maybe a modern tendency to sobriety amongst midwives had something to do with it. And what part did *le corna* play? My mind was clouded with fantasy and fear, and a growing sense of doom about the creature that was swimming in C's protuberant belly. It kicked now, frequently – a strange, glutinous, slow-motion kick that raised misshapen lumps in her flesh – and I wondered whether these were desperate signals for help. What was going on in there? And who was sending us these signals? Was it male or female, was it monstrous or normal, was it birthmarked or unblemished? Excluded by his sex from this female ritual, Oreste had waited anxiously below while his wife sweated and struggled under the hands of the drunken midwife. But judging by the gestures he was now making behind the old lady's back, his home-made wine had been more efficacious than any gesture against the *malocchio* or any prayer.

'Come and have a glass,' he invited us, 'and don't listen to her talk. They come out all right, more or less, and there's nothing much to be done about it anyway.' The fatalism of the Italian *contadino*, efficacious against any disaster.

'Perfectly satisfactory!' said Doctor Bianchi, glancing up over the great mound of pregnancy. 'We will just let things run their natural course. Plenty of time. The first child is often a bit slow in coming.'

'But we've got people coming over for the baptism.'

'That's a bit premature, isn't it?'

'They have to book flights, get time off work, that kind of thing. How long might it take?'

'My dear *signora*, this is not a factory, this is nature.'

'So you don't know?'

Doctor Bianchi, a massive, shambling figure of a man, a prop-forward in the front line of obstetrics, shrugged. 'We are all in the hand of God.'

But at the examination a few days later the waters burst – a biblical inundation – and the hospital was forced to admit her. C betrayed an expression of faint satisfaction that dates were about to be met, that booked flights could be confirmed by relatives and friends coming for the baptism, that her own timing had defeated the ineffable rhythms of nature.

They put her on a drip and connected her to electronic machinery while I paced the corridor outside along with another expectant father. This was the only establishment in the whole peninsula where No Smoking rules were enforced: my fellow sufferer was driven to skulk beyond the glass doors marked *MATERNITÀ* and puff smoke out of a window. Both of us, smoker and non-smoker, felt like insolent schoolboys called before the authorities.

'I want to be with my wife during the birth,' I told one of the nurses. 'She wants me to be there.'

The nurse smiled charmingly.

'In England it would be allowed.'

Her smile was still charming, but tinged with scepticism. She led me into the labour room. 'Five minutes,' she warned.

C smiled at me reassuringly from a bed by over by the window, as though I were the one facing the trial. A drip bottle hung over her. She was connected up to electronic machinery which blinked at me and drew traces on a screen. It looked like hi-fi equipment, which, I suppose, is more or less what it was.

'Listen,' the nurse said. 'The baby's heartbeat.'

I listened. A rippling sound came from one of the electronic boxes. The sound galloped away in the distance, a cavalry charge far away on some ringing plain, a mystery from beyond the womb. Where, I wondered, was it headed?

'Now you must go.'

'Can't I stay?'

'You must go.' A hand eased me towards the door.

'Don't worry,' said C from the bed. 'I'm all right.'

The waiting went on. I repeated my request to be present at the birth and this time a doctor came to see me. He shrugged when I asked. 'We'll see what can be done. It depends whether the *primario* is on duty or not. He doesn't like outsiders.'

'I'm not an outsider!'

He smiled sympathetically. 'We are a bit behind the times in that kind of thing.'

By now it was late afternoon and, despite the drip, contractions had not really begun. I got in to see C once more, then another nurse took me aside.

'You might as well go home,' she advised. 'It's getting late and nothing's going to happen until the morning.'

'I can wait here.'

'There's no point.'

I went in to say goodbye. There was another woman in there now, moaning and wailing and calling for her mother.

'Sorry about your company,' I said to C.

She smiled. 'She's a cousin of the pharmacist in Avea.' Of course. 'She's quite sweet in between contractions.'

'And you?'

A little shrug beneath the sheet. 'Nothing, really. The first pains, I suppose, but nothing much.'

'They told me I might as well go. Nothing will happen until the morning.'

'That's right.'

'You've got Grazia's telephone number?'

'I've already given it to them.'

So I drove home alone, wondering how C was doing in her white room surrounded by electronic machinery, wondering how the cavalry charge was going on that distant battleground.

Supper alone was a sorry affair, haunted by an absent figure and the remarkable thought that if all went well the next time C was here we would have acquired the ultimate piece of family luggage, and life would be irrevocably changed.

My meal was interrupted by a ring at the door. I opened it to find Giuseppina's husband standing in the shadows of the landing.

'*Auguri*,' he announced. Congratulations.

'?'

'*Un bel maschietto.*' A lovely boy.

'?'

'They're both fine.' He shrugged. 'It was a caesarean, but they're both fine. They phoned a cousin of mine,' he added by way of explanation, which was no explanation at all.

'But . . .' A bottle of *spumante* was thrust into my hands. '*Tutto va bene*,' he assured me, before retreating down the stairs. I was left holding the baby.

I ran up to Grazia's flat. 'Haven't they phoned?'

'Who?' she asked.

'The hospital, of course.'

She shrugged.

'Giuseppina's husband has just been here. He said it's just happened. It's a boy.' I suddenly doubted my own sanity. I held out the bottle of *spumante* as evidence that it was not all the product of a fevered brain. 'Look,' I said. She frowned at the bottle, as though it was evidence not of sanity but of inebriation. 'I must phone the hospital,' I insisted.

She led me in and pointed to the phone. I grabbed the receiver and put it to my ear. It was silent.

'It's dead,' I said.

Her eyes widened. '*Morto?*'

'Not the baby, the phone! It doesn't work.' I jiggled the carriage. 'It's not working.'

She looked relieved. 'Give it to me.' But she had no more success with the thing. '*Mortacci loro. Bastardi.*' Then

161

understanding dawned. 'They rang Giuseppina to tell you.'

'So it's true. A boy.'

'A boy.' Grazia's eyes glistened.

'A caesarean birth,' I told her. 'But it's all right.'

'*Parto cesario*?'

'It's all right. They're both all right.'

Tears began to course down Grazia's cheeks. '*Parto cesario*,' she repeated.

I ran down the stairs and out into the night to go and tell Ugo and Margaret, the *bergamasco* medical student and his wife. We rang the hospital from a call box nearby and later put the story together from that call and C's own evidence. It went like this: shortly after I had gone home the doctor on duty decided that the desperate cavalry charge, the baby's heartbeat, was faltering.

'We ought not to wait,' he said. 'For the baby's sake. We ought to deliver it by caesarean.'

'Do anything,' C replied, 'as long as you save the baby.'

So they rushed her upstairs to the operating theatre while a nurse hunted for a bottle of nail-varnish remover. 'The *primario* is on duty. He'll never allow you into the theatre with nail varnish.'

It seemed that the hospital was a little island of obeyed regulations in an ocean of evasion and contravention. NO SMOKING; NO NAIL VARNISH; NO HUS-BANDS. The acetone was found and the offending finger-nails were scrubbed clean. Actually this is not a mindless rule: it has something to do with the anaesthesia, being able to check for any blueing of the patient's fingernails through lack of oxygen, but even so when did matters of life and death ever worry an Italian bent on evading a regulation?

'Her toes,' one of the nurses whispered. 'She's got varnish on her toenails.'

'Cover them up,' the other replied, giggling. 'He'll never notice them.'

With a regulation finally evaded, they swept C into surgery and within minutes, with C on the borders of anaesthetic sleep but still aware of people around her, the baby was from his mother's womb most timely ripped.

'*Un bel maschietto*,' C heard them say. Then, 'Go and phone the father.'

They were still tidying up when the messenger returned. 'That number you gave. I can't get through. The phone doesn't work.'

There was a hasty consultation. 'Where is the *signora* from?'

'Malta.'

'Here, I mean. Where does she live?'

'Avea,' said C from the table.

'Avea. Anyone know anybody in Avea?'

One of the nurses did. Her cousin – of course – was married to a plumber in the village. 'Then ring her up and tell her.'

Village gossip is more efficient by far than SIP, the Italian telephone system. The plumber's wife was contacted and informed that *una straniera* who lived in Avea had just given birth to a baby boy. Her husband was an Englishman. Could he be informed? 'Those must be the *stranieri* living below the Rossi,' said the plumber's wife. 'You know. Ring Giuseppina.'

So they rang Giuseppina, and so Giuseppina's husband arrived on my doorstep with the story exactly right, no embellishment, no error of fact or interpretation, and a bottle of *spumante* to boot. It is not only more efficient than SIP, it's a lot more human.

Two days later, equipped with a certificate signed by the presiding midwife, I registered a new citizen of the Italian State at the public register. No one had told me that you needed to go equipped with two witnesses, so the registrar drafted in the cleaning lady and someone from the office next door. As I signed the entry I had the curious and vivid sensation that I was my own grandfather, and the child I was registering was my father. I offer that only as a piece of evidence that childbirth does curious things, even to the father who is excluded from it all.

In Italy it is now the father's right to be present at the birth of his child. It is his *constitutional* right, so the story goes, as decreed by the Constitutional Court. Like most countries in the world Italy has a constitution and amongst other things this constitution lays down the essential equality of men and women in the Republic, and so the Constitutional Court decided, quite logically, that if a woman is allowed to be present at the birth of her child (and modern medicine has not yet come up with a way of avoiding this), then so too must a man be. Simple.

This principle of equality of the sexes has had another and more bizarre effect. On any Italian beach you will see many ladies baring their breasts to the world. They do it when and as they wish and nobody gives them a second glance – well, that's not quite true, but the glances are appreciative and received in the manner they are intended, for on the whole Italian women like being looked at. This is particularly suited to Pippo's taste, for he is off to the beach at Fregene almost every day during the summer and he comes back to regale us with the sights.

'*Belle tette!*' he exclaims, cupping his hands beneath what, in all honesty, must constitute a fairly fine pair of male tits. 'Naked women everywhere.' He nods his head and grins that particular grin which is only a fraction away from a licking of the lips.

The story goes that the reason for all this bare breastedness is also constitutional, another ruling by the Constitutional Court on the basis of sexual equality. It seems that a few years ago a prominent Rome lawyer had a prominent young daughter who took to liberation and topless bathing on a prominent Rome beach. Enter the flat-footed guardians of the law and public decency, to arrest her for indecent exposure. Her incensed father took the matter to court and finally obtained a judgement from the highest court in the land: if men are allowed to bathe topless, then so too must women be. I'll bet the high-minded founding fathers of the Republic never thought of that.

# 15

One afternoon in autumn a lorry, not Pippo's, was manoeuvring laboriously in the road outside the flat when it backed into
a street lamp. Simultaneity gave no clue: outside, the roaring
of a lorry's engine and the yelling of a car driver who had been
momentarily blocked, and then the concussion of coachwork
against concrete lighting standard; inside, a sudden silence
from the refrigerator.

'*Maledizione!*'

'*Vaffanculo!*'

'*Mortacci tuoi!*'

C went out on to the front balcony to see what all the fuss
was about. The baby slept on. Down in the street the lorry
was halfway up the pavement with a street lamp emerging at
an angle from beneath its rear end. The driver climbed out
and examined it morosely.

'Get out of the way!' the driver of the blocked car yelled.
'I've got work to do.'

The lorry driver shrugged with the intense fatalism of the
Italian. Knocking a street lamp sideways was a natural
phenomenon like hurricanes or earthquakes. No *blame* could
possibly attach.

'Oh!' shouted the car driver. 'Looking for your brains?'

The lorry driver responded with spirit. '*A stronzo!*' Then
he climbed back into his cab and started the engine. As his
vehicle ground away from the pavement the lighting standard
rose up gracefully to a compromise position between its original vertical and the drunken angle to which the truck had
pushed it. C watched the lorry exit from the scene in a cloud

of black exhaust smoke and then returned to the peace and tranquillity of domestic life. Although she did not realise it at once, it was an extra peace – the refrigerator was still silent. But then refrigerators have a thermostat and they do go silent from time to time. Yet the oven light was off as well and the bottle warmer wasn't working. Neither, when she came to test them, were the lights. In the bathroom the pilot light on the water heater no longer gleamed.

She checked the trip switches outside on the landing, but they were all on. Later she went upstairs to speak to Grazia. Maybe *she* knew.

'*Quel maledetto camion.*'

'The lorry?' The connection seemed remote.

'The one that hit the street lamp,' Grazia explained. 'All the street lights are off.' To Grazia it all seemed obvious. The street lights were off – so too was our own electricity supply. I suppose it does have a degree of logic about it. It also explained why we had no electricity contract and no electricity bills: the Palazzo Rossi had been plugged into the public lighting system.

That evening we were plunged into mediaeval gloom at six o'clock. The baby wailed in the darkness. The fridge was slowly warming up to arrive at the same temperature that the oven had just reached from the other direction. C stormed upstairs, waving a torch.

'But we've got a baby!' she protested. 'What are we going to do? How am I going to prepare his bottles and wash him and his clothes? And we've got guests coming. From England,' she added as though that somehow made them threatening. 'What are you going to do?' she demanded of Pippo.

The solution, of course, was at hand. On the ground floor immediately below our flat was a small office. They sold rather inadequate financial advice to local men of business and of course they had a proper electricity supply, complete with meter and bills from the electricity company and that kind of thing. Maybe Pippo looked on them as a kind of insurance, a back-up system.

He went down to have a word with them and returned to us with an expression of the purest self-satisfaction. '*Tutt' a posto.*'

'What's happened?'

He held up an imperious finger. 'Come.' By torchlight we followed him down to the kitchen of our flat. He went out on to the side balcony and leaned over into the darkness. There were muttered voices from below.

'*Dai, dai,*' he called.

Something flashed upwards, like a fish surfacing from the depths of the ocean, a long, sinuous eel perhaps. Pippo made a grab, missed, and the eel disappeared back into the deep.

Whatever it was possessed ancestry which could be wished to perdition: '*Mortacci tuoi!*' he exclaimed. 'Try again.'

There was further muttering below and then another eel-like flash in the gloom. This time Pippo grabbed the beast by the throat.

'*Ecco!*' He turned in triumph and displayed a length of electric cable with a plug on the end. '*La corrente.*' He made an explicit gesture with the plug, as of insertion. Grazia winced. In a moment the plug was in place in a wall socket and at once there was a mutter from the refrigerator in the corner. Grazia threw the wall switches and the lights came on. The pilot light on the oven gleamed like an albino eye.

'*Voilà!*' Pippo exclaimed, as though to display bilingualism amongst his many talents. He had the manner of a conjuror displaying whole and undamaged your ten-thousand-lire note which a moment before had been torn into little pieces before your eyes. But hubris earns its own rewards: even as he spread out his arms in triumph, the whole room plunged back into darkness. The refrigerator muttered in despair and fell silent.

'*Vaffanculo!*' the disembodied voice of the conjuror shouted.

'*Madonna porca miseria! Cristo e tutti santi* . . .' Blasphemy, like poetry, is that which is lost in translation. Further expletives drifted up from the depths below the balcony and there was a hasty consultation between landlord above and tenants underneath.

'What have you got turned on?' he called to us.

'The oven,' replied a shadow nearby. 'I was baking something when the current went. And the water heater, I suppose.'

We went to turn off switches, and then waited breathless in the darkness while the people from the office below scrabbled around inside the box of trip switches at the bottom of the stairwell. Abruptly the lights returned, along with the muttering of the refrigerator, but no longer with the baleful eye of the oven.

'*Ecco,*' Pippo said cautiously, abjuring unlucky French for more mundane Italian. 'Just don't put too much on at once,' he warned. 'They've only got three kilowatts downstairs. And,' he added darkly, 'check occasionally to see if the cable is getting hot.'

There remained only the problem of the Rossi themselves, but then Grazia hadn't got a baby to serve and so she didn't really count in Pippo's eyes. A further cable was lowered from their balcony and plugged into one of our sockets. This arrangement was rather more conventional – instead of plugging this cable into their own circuit and thereby straining the office's supply beyond hope, the Rossis had nothing more than a light bulb on the end. Denied the gift of fertility, Grazia had to make do with a glaring 100-watt bulb on a long flex until such time as the curious machinations of communal electricity could restore the lighting to Via Roma and, indirectly and unintentionally, to the Palazzo Rossi. Whenever she wanted to turn the lights on she had to call down to us in the flat below. 'Stick it in!' she'd shout, as well she might.

Never, in all the time we lived in the Palazzo Rossi, did we receive a bill for the electricity we consumed. Every month, dutifully, C paid Pippo her estimate and received his signature, and laughter, in return.

Don Anastasio had a cramped office tucked up a staircase beside the parish church. There was a portrait of the Pope and a crucifix on the wall, and in a niche a rosary-draped plaster statue of Our Lady. The priest's desk was piled high with papers – mass sheets, letters with episcopal arms on the letterhead, booklets with photographs of missions in Africa, a list of names of the current catechumens, a notice for posting in the church about a pilgrimage to Assisi, notes for a sermon delivered three Sundays before, and, finally and triumphantly, his diary. He leafed through to the date we had mentioned.

'During morning mass?' he asked. 'It's better that way.'

'Of course. Although none of the guests will understand a thing.'

A shrug. 'The Lord understands.' He fiddled around with a pen that wouldn't write. 'And the name?'

'Matthew.' We enunciated it with care. '*Matthew*.'

The pen spluttered ink across a piece of scrap paper and then began to write with more assurance.

'How is it?'

We spelt it for him. 'M–A–T–T–H–E–W.'

'Mafoo,' he said hopelessly. The dental fricative plays no part in the Italian language. Don Arcangelo's tongue floundered round his teeth in a vain endeavour to get at the sound. 'Madge-you' was the nearest he could manage, and barely even that. He gave up in despair.

'It's *Matteo*, isn't it? We're in Italy: I'll call him Matteo. What does it matter? *Il buon Dio* understands Italian perfectly well. And the other names I don't even have to mention. We'll just put them in the register.'

We agreed. Matteo it would be. He wrote the details down in an ornate script. 'And the *padrini*?'

Pippo had offered his services as godfather but we had declined with regret. 'Friends from England,' we told Don Anastasio.

'They are *cristiani*?'

'*Cattolici*.'

He smiled at his slip. '*Cattolici. Bene*. We'll get their names when they sign the register. Now, a glass of something?'

Weighed down as it was with parish registers, the wooden cupboard in the corner yielded not only more paperwork but a bottle of Johnny Walker and three glasses. Black Label. There are few material comforts for a parish priest in any country in the world and certainly not in village Italy. At least the whisky was good quality.

'*Un brindisi*,' Don Anastasio suggested, raising his glass. Quite why the word for a toast should be the name of a southern Italian seaport I have never been able to discover. '*A* Madge-you,' the priest said gamely.

'*A Matteo*,' we answered. Don Anastasio laughed.

Thus it was that before an Italian-speaking God and a congregation which included such diverse beings as a female partner in an Italian plastics firm, a retired Royal Air Force officer, a research geophysicist of South African origin, an illiterate Italian property owner, a Bergamask medical student, a Belgian geographer, a couple of English teachers, a Maltese secretary, and sundry villagers, Matthew was admitted into the congregation of the Lord – and if he ever wishes to get married according to the rites of Holy Mother Church I foresee one devil of a job persuading whom it may concern that Matthew of the birth certificate is Matteo of the baptism document. It's the kind of thing which renders Italian bureaucracy catatonic. He'll probably have to get a notary public to witness his solemn declaration that the two are in fact one.

'But he's not Matteo,' his grandmother protested when she discovered the fact. 'He's English!'

'He's half-Maltese,' C reminded her.

The question is a subtle one. He is, I suspect, whole Italian.

We decamped from the church to a restaurant just outside the village for lunch. The meal included wild-boar stew and much red wine and Pippo – resplendent in white silk suit – posed for photographs with his head thrown back and the christening cake held aloft as though he were about to take part in the custard-pie sequence of a slapstick film. He did have a certain resemblance to Oliver Hardy. At another table was a small wedding party. The bride was magnificently pregnant beneath her white dress. We all toasted the baby that already was and the baby that was to be. Later on that afternoon my father and Pippo slumped in armchairs in the sitting room of the flat.

'I too was in the air force,' Pippo declared. 'During the war.'

The remark was duly translated. My father looked impressed. *'Io in Italia,'* he explained, struggling nobly with the language. 'Monopoli, Napoli, Roma.'

'*Io a Rodi,*' Pippo responded, getting into the swing of things.

'What's a *rodi?*' Father asked.

'Rhodes. The island.'

'Oh, Rhodes.' He smiled and nodded at our landlord. '*Io* bombed – how do you say "bombed"?'

I winced. '*Ho bombardato.*'

'*Bombardato. Io bombardato Rodi.*'

Pippo nodded. He didn't seem put out. My mind gave me a picture of Pippo in shabby uniform skulking in a foxhole while my father flew overhead in his Wellington and tried to blow the poor man to bits.

'*Poi son' andato a Bari.*'

'Bari?' my father asked with growing enthusiasm.

'Bari,' I admitted.

'I bombed Bari too. *Bombardato Bari*' – a new word slipped into the front of his mind – '*anche.*' Also.

Pippo looked most impressed. '*Poi son' andato a Livorno.*'

'And Livorno.' Father's command of the language was growing by the minute. '*Ho bombardato Livorno. Anche.*' It seemed that his war had been personally directed at the wretched Pippo. My father appeared to have chased my future landlord round half the Mediterranean theatre trying to drop bombs on him. Feeling sorry for Pippo was a new experience.

'He also sent supplies to the partisans,' I put in desperately, not knowing how to say it in correct Italian. '*Ha paracaduto ai partigiani.*'

Pippo looked even more impressed and I had a suspicion that I had got it wrong. Did Pippo imagine my father himself, having failed with the bombing, now dropping through the night sky to come and get him? I tried to explain. '*Non lui. La roba, ai partigiani.*'

'Tell him about Bambino,' Father said. It was a story he'd told me before, the agent with the code-name Bambino whom they had dropped into lago di Lesina in the Gargano peninsula – just a courageous little man being launched into the void to fight his own bitterly dangerous and completely forgotten war amongst his own people: the merest footnote in history. 'Tell him about Bambino,' Father insisted. *'Un bon Italiano,'* he added for Pippo's sake. Thinking that the words referred to him, Pippo grinned expansively and puffed out his chest.

'Tell him about Bambino.'

'It would only muddle things up. They're muddled enough as it is. He'd probably end up thinking you dropped a baby into the lake.'

'Where did he go after Livorno, then?'

'Do you want to see if you bombed that as well?'

'It might be interesting. Serve him right for not putting central heating in the flat as he promised.'

'I don't think things can serve you right forty years in advance of the wrong.'

Pippo watched us with interest, eternally amazed that foreigners actually understood each other.

*'Dopo Livorno?'* Father asked innocently.

*'Dopo Livorno niente. Era la fine.'* After Livorno was the end. Unexpectedly, one might say against all the odds, there was a strange dignity about the man. 'After Livorno,' he said, 'I walked home.' Then he brightened up. *'La fine della guerra!'* he exclaimed with feeling. He picked up his glass – we had opened a bottle of brandy – and raised it in a toast. *'Un brindisi!'* he proposed.

Father nodded. 'And Brindisi,' he said with a certain gloomy satisfaction. 'I bombed Brindisi too.'

It was not long after our guests had returned to England that Pippo had his next baptism. This was some relative or other and all it meant to us was a Sunday without the continuous noise of people tramping back and forth above our heads. For a few hours we could imagine ourselves alone while the baby grinned and gurgled at us.

Then in the early evening a roar of Alfa Romeo in the street outside announced the return of the *padrone*. We heard their footsteps on the stairs, and Pippo's voice bellowing in the stairwell. We waited with bated breath for them to pass by our front door and continue up to their flat. The footsteps came nearer, reached the landing outside, went past our door. We breathed relief. Then the door bell rang.

I groaned. 'What does he want now?'

C opened the door to them.

'Shhhh!' said Grazia to her consort. 'The baby.'

C missed her cue. 'He's not asleep. I'm just preparing his food.'

'Can we see him?'

They came in, Pippo distinctly the worse for wear. His silk tie was askew, his shirt and jacket crumpled. There were gravy stains down his front.

'*Un battesimo,*' he announced. '*Io sono il padrino.*' Padrino may mean godfather but it has other connotations in Italian, those same connotations that, thanks to Francis Ford Coppola and Marlon Brando, the word godfather has also acquired in English. And he did look like some kind of Mafia godfather standing there in the kitchen with his white suit and co-respondent shoes. '*Il padrino,*' he repeated.

He sat down rather suddenly, eyes rolling lugubriously. '*Quindici litri,*' he exclaimed in surprise.

'Fifteen litres of what?' C asked.

'*Vino.*' He belched. 'With a friend, a *cugino*, the other *padrino. Quindici litri.*'

Grazia had picked the baby up and was cooing to it in Neapolitan. She glanced anxiously at Pippo as he sat there at the table balancing his head on his shoulders.

'*Quindici litri. Bevo io, bevi tu; bevo io, bevi tu.*' I drink, you drink. He pointed as he said it, just in case we hadn't got the point: his thumb towards his mouth, then his forefinger pointing at the imaginary drinking partner. '*Bevo io, bevi tu; bevo io, bevi tu. Quindici litri.*'

'Too much,' said Grazia laconically.

'*Quindici litri,*' came the mournful cry from the crumpled

figure at the table. '*Bevo io, bevi tu; bevo io, bevi tu. Fa male.*'
It hurts. Quite what hurt was not entirely clear, but it was
certain enough that something did.

'Would you like some bicarbonate, Pippo?' C asked sooth-
ingly.

Pippo thought that a grand idea. '*Quindici litri,*' he
mumbled. It was no longer a boast, more a confession, with
penance yet to do. The bicarbonate of soda fizzed before his
eyes, beaded bubbles winking at the brim.

'*Sta' attento,*' Grazia warned.

Pippo raised the cup and drank. There was a pause like the
lull before the storm, like the strange silence that precedes, so
they say, the earthquake. Then suddenly he was gone. The
door to the bathroom slammed. We sat in the kitchen in silence
and heard only splashing noises, a Niagara of sound, a flood.

'*Che cretino!*' Grazia cried, handing the baby back to its
mother. She went after the wretched Pippo and her voice was
raised in fury.

'I'm not surprised,' C said mildly. 'I mean, fifteen litres!'

'All over the bathroom,' I observed.

# 16

In winter, towards Christmas, the circus came to town. Moribund if not actually dead in Britain, the travelling circus, with its caged beasts, its caravans, its striped tent inching upwards one afternoon over a convenient piece of waste ground, is still part of Italian village life. The *comune* contributes its bit by laying on free electricity.

'Probably plugged into the street-lighting supply,' I suggested.

From our rear balcony we watched them hoist the big top. It was a fine sight, an inverted bowl of blue, red and white stripes with the name in lights at the summit: CIRCO ERASMO. All around was a muddy waste ground where bits of ironmongery lay rusting amongst the nettles: an old band saw, a wrecked Fiat 500 amongst the stinging nettles, a pile of ancient bed frames, that kind of thing. They parked the caravans there and hung out their washing and lit their stoves and humped bales of straw about the place. A group went round the village posting bills. Over cards in the Bar Rasenna the old men muttered about thieves and mountebanks, while down in the valley below the *centro storico* the children hung around the edge of the encampment and gawped.

Next day the circus paraded through the streets of the *paese*. A truck led the way with three sequinned ladies standing in the back, waving and grinning at the villagers. It was followed by a moth-eaten camel and a liberally defecating elephant. Then there were two plumed horses and, finally, a flock of dogs. Occasionally their handler could persuade them on to their hind legs, which was where they were meant to be, but more often they scurried round on all fours, straining at their leashes to get at any available bit of canine tail Avea might offer. Leading this motley procession was the ringmaster, resplendent in tailcoat and top hat.

'This evening, for your delight,' he cried, 'the Circo Erasmo! Ferocious lions! Man-eating crocodiles! Exotic elephants!' – the great pile of excrement in the middle of the road rather belied that assertion – 'death-defying trapeze artistes, hilarious clowns, fire-eaters, jugglers, all the fun of the circus! Two performances this evening! Don't miss . . .' etcetera, etcetera. In between the items of his announcement canned music shrieked out through a barrier of electronic distortion and feedback. The Aveani watched shrewdly, gathered up the elephant's excrement to use as manure on the *orto*, reserved their judgement.

We took the baby for a walk down into the valley past the encampment. The smell of caged animal was strong. It had been raining earlier and the occasional figure plodded morosely through the mud between one gleaming silver caravan and another. There was that gypsy air of mystery about the place, the sense of unease which hangs round the edges of travelling folk. C, a child of the Mediterranean, tucked the baby more firmly into his pram lest quick hands should steal him away. 'You never know,' she asserted, irrefutably.

As we passed, a woman emerged from one of the nearest caravans to fling a bucket of water into the bushes. She was dressed in black – shapeless black sweater, baggy black trousers, black wellington boots. Juggler? Contortionist? Trapeze artiste? There was no means of telling. Perhaps she wore pillows and did the circus fat lady. All things seemed possible.

'Maybe we ought to come this evening,' I suggested to C. 'You don't see travelling circuses these days in England.'

'What would we do with the baby?'

'Bring him too.'

As we spoke the woman turned and looked at us, her hands planted firmly on her hips. I nodded to her and attempted a smile. There was something threatening about her appearance, and nothing whatever that one might have associated with one of the glittering beauties waving at Avea from the back of a truck earlier in the day. A cloud of frantic black hair framed a pallid face. Her lips were crimson, like a splash of blood.

'Ooo, you're English!' she cried. 'What the 'ell are you doing 'ere?' In the shadow of Avea's old walls, in the encampment of Circo Erasmo, the accent was pure Birmingham.

'We live here.'

'Well, fancy that!'

'And you,' I asked, with what I considered greater justification, 'what are *you* doing here?'

'Me? I work here. I say, you don't fancy coming in for a cuppa tea, do you? It's ever so nice to hear English. All these wops, very nice I'm sure, but they do get on your nerves, if you know what I mean.'

'But what work do you do?' I asked.

'What do I do?' She shrugged as though it was obvious. 'I wrestle with crocodiles.'

We made our way through the mud towards the door of her

179

caravan. She cooed at the baby and showed us where to leave our shoes and ushered us into the chromium-plated monster.

'Do you want to bring the pram in? Suit yourselves. I'll just pop the kettle on. Lovely to be able to speak a bit of English with someone. Make yourself comfortable.' We might have been visiting a terrace house in Sutton Coldfield rather than a circus caravan in central Italy belonging to a lady crocodile wrestler. She took C's confession of Latin blood with resignation. 'There's a lot of it about, dear. It can't be helped.'

'How long have you been in Italy?' I asked.

The woman shrieked with laughter at the idea. 'We're not really *in* Italy, love. We're in the circus, know what I mean? Here today, middle of next week tomorrow, that sort of thing. Now you make yourselves comfortable in the parlour while I get things ready. Nothing special, mind you, at this short notice, but it's nice to have a bit of a chat. I'm sure I've got some cake.'

We made our way towards the bay windows at the end of the caravan. The vehicle had concertina bits which enabled it to swell out when parked and the living area was spacious and shining, a shrine in velvet plush and chrome and imitation wood veneer. The object of the shrine was the crocodile. There were crocodiles everywhere – crocodiles pictured on the wall, crocodiles figured in china on the shelves, crocodiles embroidered into cushions, crocodiles carved in wood, crocodiles cast in metal. There were also, on the lady's dainty feet, crocodile-skin slippers.

'No false sentiment, love,' she explained when she saw my glance. 'They're murdering bastards. I'm Madame Nefertiti, the crocodile tamer from Luxor. Did you see the posters? Luxor's in Egypt, you know. Actually the crocs come from Florida but I think Luxor has a lot more class, don't you?'

'And you actually wrestle with them?'

'Oh yes, dear. No mucking about. I *writhe* all over the place with them, all done up in my sequins and leotard. Quite an act it is.' Her teapot was aquamarine, with a crocodile on the side. Only the cups were crocodile-free. They were trimmed with pink and had a garland of flowers for handles, the kind of thing you might win as a prize in a fairground. 'You'll want milk with it, I suppose? All this lemon stuff you get here – no wonder, I always say, no wonder. Although the milk's not like England, is it?'

'And how long have you been doing the act?'

Madame Nefertiti considered my question for a moment, caught in the act of passing round sponge cake. 'Let me see. I started as a juggler when I was six. That was my grandpa's act. Go on, dear, help yourself, it's home-made. *Pan di Spagna*, they call it here, for heaven's sake. Can't get more English than sponge cake, can you? Where was I? Oh yes, The Incredible Masons, that was our name. Fairground stuff and the odd circus. Did a bit of trapeze work and then I went into contortion. You've got to start early with that, when your joints are still supple. Still tie me feet round me back occasionally, I do. That was The Knot Girl. Lots of skills in this business, you know. Got to 'ave 'em, really, otherwise you get stale. I was The Knot Girl for about three years before I met my husband. Still do a bit nowadays, matter of fact.'

'Was he circus, your husband?'

She smiled wryly. 'You don't meet much else, love. The Amazing Amazon, I became. Wouldn't believe it to look at me. He was a strongman, you know the kind of thing? All bending bars and lifting people up by one finger and that kind of thing. He used to throw me round something frightful. I got a bit fed up with that so we went for the animal act, be about fifteen years ago now. Stole it off a Romanian couple, actually.'

'Stole it?'

'The idea, not the crocs. More cake? Go on, it'll only go stale. We was Tarzan and Jane, the Children of the Jungle at first. Not very imaginative name, I know, but we did well enough. The crocs were something a bit different, I suppose.

181

Even did one season at Billy Smart's. You might have seen us on telly.' She paused. 'And then he had his accident.'

Accident. We sat among the teacups, the signs of suburban banality, and contemplated the word. With the utmost delicacy Madame Nefertiti used blood-red talons to remove a crumb from her blood-red lower lip. 'The muscles which open their jaws are very weak,' she said. 'You can hold them closed with just one hand. But the muscles which close them are something different . . .'

C put her cup down. We had brought in the carrycot part of the pram and the baby was beginning to make the grunting noise which signified hunger.

'Little darling,' said Madame Nefertiti as C rocked him.

'What happened?' I asked.

'Lost an arm,' she said flatly. 'Couldn't go on after that, could he? The One-Armed Tarzan? Doesn't sound too good, does it? Like a fire-eater with third-degree burns.' She shrieked with laughter. 'So I had to go it alone, and we had to change the act a bit.'

'You didn't think of getting rid of the animals?'

'The crocs? Oh, Lord no. It'd be like biting the hand that feeds you.' Her slight frame shook with laughter. 'That's a good one, isn't it? The hand that feeds you. Ooo, I haven't had such a good laugh in years. And you,' she asked when the laughter had been brought under control, 'what do you do?'

'I'm a teacher,' I said lamely.

We emerged from the caravan into a wet December afternoon. The shabby walls of Avea, ancient, decaying, at times mysterious and always fascinating, loomed over us. But somehow they seemed rather mundane beside the woman in black who wrestled with crocodiles and lived the life of a traveller, a life set aslant from ours and informed with a strange evanescence, a vivid sense of the ephemeral nature of being.

'Hope you'll come to the performance. 'Ere, show 'em this and you'll get a reduction.'

We took the complimentary slip. 'Of course we will.'

'Lovely seeing you,' she called as we splashed away through the mud. 'Bloody weather, isn't it? This is the last stop before we pack it in for the winter. Left it bloody late, if you ask me.'

She stood silhouetted in the doorway to her caravan. In a moment she would be back inside, pouring herself into sequined leotard and tights and bundling her hair into Queen Nefertiti's tall headdress. Her one-armed husband would be stirring the crocodiles round with a fork or whatever one did. The first show of the evening would be about to begin.

'I thought Pippo was strange until I met her,' I said to C as we climbed the hill away from the circus tent.

'I thought she was very ordinary,' C replied.

'That's what was so strange.'

In the darkness of a December evening the circus was a garish focus, a hub round which the village revolved for a few hours. Brassy music, the peculiar mechanical sound of some kind of organ, sprayed out into the darkness from a battery of loudspeakers. Lights glittered round the name board across the summit of the big top. A voice boomed into the night calling the faithful to prayer.

Pippo did not heed the call. He was at home watching television, zapping with the remote control.

'We're going to the circus,' we told him.

He pursed his lips lasciviously, almost interested. 'The women,' he said, gesturing with cupped hands. 'Big tits.'

'One of them wrestles with crocodiles,' we revealed, and Pippo's eyes rolled. Surely he'd not find that on television, and never in the *flesh*. 'Why don't you come?'

He hesitated, truly he hesitated. But the circus was children's stuff and on television one didn't have to pause between acts. Although Pippo did not realise it, it was another ruling of the Constitutional Court which affected his life, almost his every waking moment – and by proxy ours beneath him: the ruling that freedom of information means precisely that, and that therefore anyone can set up a television channel. But although the Constitutional Court has power to decree that anyone can broadcast, it has no power to regulate how they should do so. Thus a kind of legally sanctioned anarchy prevails. Telelazio, Telepiù, Reteroma, Italia Uno, the names of the stations drivel on through the mind just as the programmes drivel on through the air, a mixture of third-rate films, home-grown game shows, endless advertising, and the occasional strip show. All this was to Pippo's delight. For hours he would lie in bed with the remote control in his hand, flipping from channel to channel and pausing only when he chanced on a shoot-out or a glimpse of naked female flesh. Storyline was unimportant because never in his life has Pippo watched a film from beginning to end. As we wrapped up the baby against the cold we could hear him overhead tearing the violent heart out of any film he happened upon. All he watches is the sex and violence.

We walked down to the circus through a December drizzle. At the turnstiles a thin line of worshippers stood in the mud to pay their couple of thousand lire, but all too few of the Aveani had braved the weather. The woman who took the money was vast and lightly bearded. When we displayed Madame Nefertiti's voucher she granted us a thousand-lire reduction, but then she seemed to grant the same to everyone else in the queue, voucher or not. Maybe the quoted price was just a bargaining position. We exchanged greetings with Maddalena and her daughter, and the girl who helped Giuseppina in the *alimentari*, and the man from the bank, and the wife of the man who kept the petrol pumps and a dozen other familiar faces.

'Better than staying at home and watching television,' I suggested. There was some doubt about the matter, some suggestion that the majority decision had been the better one. Inside the big top it was warm and bright and damp. There was the smell of crushed grass and crushed bodies and crushed hopes. A girl in a sequined bikini was selling popcorn and fizzy drinks from a stall; at the back of the ring a clown with a red ping-pong ball for a nose was fiddling rather disconsolately with a loudspeaker.

We took our seats near the ringside and had barely settled when, with a shriek like the wailing of the souls in hell, Madame Nefertiti advanced on us from behind the popcorn. People turned to watch.

''Ello dears! Lovely to see you! Do hope you enjoy it all.' She embraced C and kissed the baby as though greeting old friends. 'Oooo, i'n't 'e lovely? What a little darling!' The sound of Birmingham had been incongruous enough in the muddy encampment in the afternoon: inside the big top it seemed outrageous.

Pippo ought to have come, I thought. Madame Nefertiti about to perform was a very different thing from Madame Nefertiti tinkling over the teapot. Her breasts leaked out over cups no bigger than Pippo's own hands. Tassels glittered and dangled over pieces of gold lamé which had been stretched to the point of surrender. Her face was carefully carved from foundation cream and rouge. She was a sensation.

'When are you on?' I asked politely, conscious of the fact that Avea was watching, that it was now probably labelling us as circus folk who had decided to go straight.

'Well, first I've got a number on me own, my contortion bit. Then I come on with me little babies. Now I'd better go. See you!'

She pranced off with a shiver of buttock as the ringmaster took the centre of the ring. There was a blast of organ music.

'*Signore, signori, benvenuto al mondo magico del circo!*'

The children squealed with delight and the performance began. First there were the dogs skipping round the ring balancing balls on their noses, occasionally dropping on all fours before a crack of the whip reminded them that this was business. Then there were some red-bottomed monkeys clinging grimly to three cantering ponies. Then the ringmaster took the microphone once more: 'And now let's hear your applause for *il Groviglio Umano, la Signorina dei Nodi . . .*'

Of course it was Madame Nefertiti. The audience held its collective breath as she wrapped herself into her own limbs and walked round the ring on her hands with her chin resting on her buttocks. When it became clear that she wouldn't actually come to pieces they laughed with relief. At the end of the act she unwound slowly, like someone unpacking the best china and worrying where the pieces are.

'*La Signorina viene dalla Persia,*' the ringmaster assured us, but as she bounced past she winked broadly. We knew she came from Sutton Coldfield. In the interval she was there again, selling popcorn. It wasn't until the end of the second half of the performance that she appeared with the crocodiles. By this time she had changed into a tunic of vaguely Egyptian inspiration and a golden headdress which was decorated with palm trees and papyrus plants. As she had promised she wallowed round in a tank full of the malign beasts, skilfully avoiding thrashing tails and expertly holding their noses as she kissed them, eventually hypnotising one of them and riding another as though it were a horse. The village children screamed with delight.

'*Madame Nefertiti, la domatrice del Nilo!*'

She stood poised with her feet on two of the largest brutes and her headdress glittering beneath the lights. Madame Nefertiti . . . and the Human Entanglement . . . and the woman who sold popcorn during the interval. A dying breed.

The next morning I had to go to work and when I got back in the afternoon the wasteland beneath the walls of the *centro storico* was empty – just an area of trampled mud with the usual pieces of iron rusting in the cold rain: an old band saw, a wrecked Fiat 500 amongst the stinging nettles, a pile of ancient bed frames. Circo Erasmo had vanished, as circuses do.

# 17

December hurried towards Christmas and the New Year. There was none of the glitter of a northern Christmas, little of that hysterical anticipation of indigestion and financial profit which starts in October and has rendered the Anglo-Saxon Christmas almost unrecognisable as a religious feast. The Christmas tree and Father Christmas and the spending binge has come slowly to Italy, but the sense of religious feast has been here ever since Christmas itself, in a typically Italian piece of pragmatism, was invented in the fourth century AD out of the pagan festival of Sol Invictus. The Italians have never been ones to indulge in fanaticism. They have always understood that nothing is simple, nothing pure, nothing perfect. Compromise is the watchword.

The traditional Christmas fair in Piazza Navona probably dates from those distant times when the Church was assimilating the pagan festivals into its calendar. Lying in the crook of the Tiber's elbow in the heart of the city, the piazza itself is quintessential old Rome. It has the ground plan of an imperial stadium, but the houses which ring it are mediaeval and renaissance in origin, built in the days when the piazza had become one of Rome's principal markets. Later the baroque period contributed the church of Sant' Agnese and a palace or two and the piazza's crowning glory, Bernini's grandiose Fountain of the Four Rivers, to create a typical Roman architectural palimpsest and one of the most celebrated pieces of public art in the world. Yet for all its grandeur, for all its showpiece quality, the piazza still has that sense of street theatre which it must have possessed when Caravaggio's mistress plied her trade there, or even earlier when it was an imperial stadium surrounded by taverns and brothels, where Sant' Agnese herself was exposed naked before a jeering crowd of youths.

'You must come to Piazza Navona,' Lorenzo insisted. 'A tradition. The Roman Christmas isn't like the American one, but we have something. You must buy figures for the crib.'

We went down in the evening and parked on the Lungotevere. The Campo Marzio area, the Campus Martius of the ancient city, is a warren of mediaeval alleys, a maze of narrow spaces and hidden corners, the *centro storico* of Avea writ large. In Imperial times it was an area of public parks, of pleasure gardens and pavilions, of baths and theatres. But now the name Campo Marzio is attached only to a baroque church, and the Pantheon, the shrine of Imperial Rome become the shrine of the united Italian kingdom, stands silent and morose in a space too small for it. Our footsteps echoed from mediaeval walls which had broken classical columns embedded into their stonework. Cats slunk from shadow to shadow and squabbled on a nearby roof. Scraps of paper tumbled along on the wind. At the Palazzo Madama, the home of the Italian senate, there were arc lights and plumed *carabinieri* on guard but they seemed like forces of occupation, a foreign power intruding on a place that was resentful of the present.

And then we broke out into the piazza. It was like the raising of a theatre curtain. The great space in front of us was brilliant with light and seething with people. It was raucous, flashy, and, as only a Roman scene can be, eternal.

'*Ecco!*' said Lorenzo, as though he had just invented it all. 'You take your pick.'

The fountain is the hub round which the market revolves. The noise of human voices mingles with the rush of falling water and you wonder whether this too, the sound as well as the sight, was part of Bernini's intention. There are artists drawing caricatures and Abruzzi shepherds playing the *zampogna* and buskers playing the violin and beggars tugging at your sleeve. Doubtless there are also *scippatori* snatching handbags and pushers trading marijuana; but mainly, herding from stall to stall, there are ordinary Roman families buying candyfloss and sweets, arguing over trinkets, bargaining for children's toys, raising their voices to protest about Christmas-tree lights, debating over figures for the crib.

The crib is the great tradition, invented, so the story goes, by Saint Francis himself at Greccio in the Sabine hills near Rieti. But he was stage-managing a *presepio vivente*, a living crib: on sale in Piazza Navona are figurines for model cribs. Two-thirds of the stalls are devoted to them, and over the centuries the thing has become a riot of non-canonical embroidery: of course there are oxen and asses and shepherds with their flocks and angels with banners saying *Gloria in Excelsis Deo* and that kind of thing; but there are also men coming back from the fields and women selling things from stalls, a baker taking bread from the oven, carters with a barrel of wine, a boy playing with his dog, a man playing the concertina, a drunk lying beneath a tree; then there are inns and markets and houses, mossy hills with caves for the holy family, windmills and water wheels which actually work, churches – yes, churches – with domes and bell-towers, in fact a whole *paesaggio* of the Italian *settecento*, through which the *Tre Re Magi* pick their way with a certain air of incongruity. All this exists amidst the usual tawdriness of a fair, but that is exactly the point – the tradition *lives*; it does not have to be preserved or revived.

'Don't accept their asking price,' Lorenzo admonished us. 'They're all crooks.'

So we bought a few pieces – Mary and Joseph and the child, two shepherds and a Wise Man, a sheep and a camel and an entirely non-kosher pig – and took them proudly back to the flat, and the collection has grown over the years. But we've never acquired a windmill that works. Later we discovered that the Colasanti family owned antique figures made of porcelain and, in an alcove in their sitting room, created a display which would have competed with the best any Roman church had to offer. Our own figurines are plastic. We console ourselves with the idea that our attempt is closer to the anarchic spirit of the people for whom cribs were intended, the illiterate and the ignorant – Pippo, in fact. When we had arranged the things and constructed some kind of stable round them, he came down to examine what we had done. He shook his head in disapprobation.

'*Che robaccia*,' he muttered.

'It's traditional.'

He shrugged. He wouldn't have given a bent fifty-lire piece for the stuff. 'Where's your soul?' we demanded, but he just laughed.

'Anyway, it's not Roman at all,' Grazia claimed just to finish off our enthusiasm. 'It's Neapolitan. You should go to Naples if you want to see the real stuff.'

'But the tradition is . . .' In vain did we try to explain about Saint Francis and his living crib in the Sabine hills.

'*Questi romani*,' she said, and the derision in her tone cut like a knife, '*questi romani non sanno che cazzo fanno.*' There is a fine euphony about the expression which is lost in translation: 'these Romans don't know what the bugger they're doing' is perhaps the sense; but *cazzo* means prick.

I didn't bother to point out that Francis was Umbrian.

*

In the parish church in the village they also had a crib, and a fine one it was too. It was a large affair erected in one of the side chapels, complete with running water piped in from the holy-water stoup nearby and a water wheel that turned and a light shining overhead like the Star of Bethlehem itself. The Wise Men were tiny figures in the distance and the shepherds were, for the moment, trying to make sense of a clutch of angels over to one side. In the stable a light flashed on and off above the empty manger as though warning the faithful that more was to come. Everything would happen in order: the shepherds would cluster round the baby Jesus only after mid-night on Christmas Eve, the Three Wise Men would only approach the cave at Epiphany.

But Don Anastasio aspired to greater things than a mere model: he wished to pursue the Franciscan original. *PRESE-PIO VIVENTE*, announced posters round the village, *ALLA VIGILIA DI NATALE*. The sponsors were, we were informed, the local bank. The whole thing was under the patronage of the *comune*.

That Christmas Eve we were invited to supper with the Rossi. We took little presents with us, but when we offered them to our hosts we found that we were standing on opposite sides of a gulf between cultures. In Italy Father Christmas has no status in popular myth. There are those who might say he has precious little such status in the Anglo-Saxon countries, being largely an invention of American nineteenth-century commercial enterprise, but in Italy he is exclusively a device, and a recent device, for supermarket windows. No Santa Claus tramps the streets or holds court in department stores or flits through the winter night to bring gifts to children, for in Italy the day for exchanging gifts is neither the Feast of Saint Nicholas on the sixth of December – this despite the fact that the good bishop's relics actually reside in Bari – nor Christmas Eve itself. In Italy the gifts come, like those of the Wise Men, on the feast of the Epiphany, and they are brought by a curious

figure whose name is a corruption of the word *epifania* itself
– La Befana.

La Befana will never make it in the world of Madison Avenue. She has none of the forced *bonhomie*, the ho! ho! ho! and happy smiles of the jolly fraud with pink cheeks and cotton-wool beard. La Befana is an ugly old crone, a witch who flies over the rooftops on her broomstick and brings sweets to the good children and lumps of charcoal to the bad. She has warts on her face and hair like straw and a bulbous, hooked nose: she is a thoroughly nasty piece of work . . . But when the State tried to connive at her disappearance by removing Epiphany from the list of public holidays (it did this by prior arrangement with the Church, which is the kind of thing that the Italians expect to happen), there was such an outcry that the holiday had to be restored. Thus democracy had its small moment of victory and the old hag still reigns supreme.

So on Christmas Eve we stood in Grazia's kitchen holding out our presents and receiving blank looks in return. Grazia's younger brother Gennaro, who had come up to stay with them over the holiday, was sitting at the kitchen table. Maddalena was hanging festoons of *fettuccini* over the backs of chairs in anticipation of dinner. Grazia was gutting fish at the sink. They turned and watched, as though we might do something dangerous.

'Where's Pippo?'

Pippo, for some reason, was in bed. We waited awkwardly while he emerged from the bedroom and came slopping down the corridor in slippers and dressing gown.

'*Buon natale*,' we said, holding his present out to him.

He grunted and took the package and examined it suspiciously, as though there might be strings attached.

'*Grazie*,' he said uncertainly.

'It's a Christmas present. Go on, open it.'

He did so, cautiously, in case the whole thing might explode. It was a small leather key-holder.

'For your house keys,' we explained. A front door had only

appeared on their apartment in the last few weeks so house keys were still a novelty. C pointed out the words on the flap. 'Greetings from Malta, it says.'

His face brightened, like Eeyore's when Piglet presented him with the burst balloon. '*Auguri da Malta*,' he said, grinning now. '*Grazie. Auguri da Malta*,' he repeated with confidence. The fact that it had words seemed to make it all the better. He could show it to his mates at the bar and explain it to them almost as though he could read English, almost as though he could read.

'And Grazia . . .'

She wiped her hands on her apron and took her present. It was wrapped in tissue paper, a handkerchief of Maltese lace with the letter G embroidered in one corner. She looked at it for a moment, then gave a little cry, flung her arms round C, and then immediately put the present to use by dabbing her eyes.

'*Un brindisi!*' she cried, and went scurrying inside a cupboard for a bottle of *spumante*. The cork came out of the bottle with no more than a faint exhalation. We raised our glasses and toasted *buon natale e buon anno* in flat, sweet *spumante*.

When Grazia announced that her brother was getting married in the spring it was an inevitable reason for another toast. Gennaro grinned and nodded as we drank. '*Auguroni!*' exclaimed Pippo. '*Auguroni da Malta*,' he added triumphantly.

'*Dove'veni*,' said the brother.

I smiled vacantly.

Gennaro pointed at me. '*Dove'veni*,' he repeated usefully.

'From England?' I hazarded, but I'd obviously got it wrong.

'*A Naboli*,' he insisted. '*A Naboli. Alle nozze.*'

'He says you must come,' Grazia explained. 'You must come to the wedding.'

'The wedding?'

'In Naples, in the spring.'

I nodded enthusiastically. 'We'll come.'

Gennaro nodded back. *'Mi biac' i stanieri,'* he said. I like foreigners.

Contact, fragile and ephemeral, had been established. *'A me piacciono gli italiani,'* I replied.

He shook his head. *'Non son' italiano. Son' nabolitano.'* Which made the unification of the country in 1870 seem a fragile thing.

Dinner involved the usual battle with mountains of *fettuccine*, and then the traditional Christmas Eve fish. We watched in awe as Grazia produced plates of eels and mackerel and *baccalà* (salt cod) and *mazzancole* (giant prawns) and cuttle-fish. Fish on Christmas Eve I had understood to be a kind of abstinence, like fish on Fridays. It appeared that it was merely an excuse for further indigestion.

*'Roba da Napoli,'* Pippo asserted. *'Magna, magna.'* His chin was daubed with sauce from the pasta; now he began to take giant prawns to pieces with his fingers, discarding their carapaces in a rancid heap. *'Son' boni!'* he exclaimed. Grazia was washing up the dishes we had used for the pasta and resisted all demands from us that she sit down. Quiet to the point of invisibility, Madalena had already slipped out of the flat.

We explained that we were going to see the *presepio vivente* later. 'Why don't you come?' we asked Pippo.

He laughed through flakes of cod and mackerel. He had seen it all before. 'I was Joseph,' he explained with pride. 'Many years ago.' He paused and gave us that look of sly delight. 'And Mary was really pregnant.'

We hardly dared breathe. 'Not you, Pippo?'

He rolled his eyes and held his finger to his lips. 'Not me . . . my cousin.'

'And did Mary . . .' I made a gesture, as of issuing forth. 'During the performance?'

He roared with laughter. His teeth were awe-inspiring in their variety of colour. 'Not then. Months later, but her parents had moved by then. To Milan or somewhere.'

194

'But you saw the baby?'

'Not saw.' He put out a hand towards C's belly and, mercifully, squeezed the air just above it. 'I could *feel* it.'

'Not during the performance?'

'When the priest wasn't looking.'

'But you're not coming this evening?'

He laughed at the suggestion. 'You go. You'll enjoy it. Me? I've seen it all before. I'll watch television instead.'

The wind blew from the north-east, clear and cold. When the wind is in that direction there is little between Italy and the Russian steppe; the air has the cutting edge of Siberia about it, the cold that killed so many of Oreste's companions-at-arms. We wrapped ourselves in scarves and stumped through the night to the *centro storico* where the faithful had gathered to witness the magical moment. The *piazzetta* outside the church door was a perfect site for the performance, and Avea was the perfect place to provide the props – a dozen bales of straw (although they had the look of the mechanical baler about them), a calf, three sheep, and a donkey. The mothers of the participants had made the costumes and a rough *capanna* had been erected beside the *comune* to act as the stable. A dozen schoolchildren had been drilled in the events of that first Christmas night of the year 5 BC, or whenever it was.

'*In quei giorni un decreto di Cesare Augusto ordinò che si facesse il censimento di tutta la terra,*' piped up a small voice.

The audience stamped its feet and huddled into scarves and hoods. Mary's pale face gazed out from the depths of a woollen shawl, Joseph's nose was running profusely, and – decidedly non-canonical, this – there was a deacon of the Roman Catholic Church in attendance, ordering the players about, beckoning the shepherds forward with their mindless sheep and sending the Three Wise Men back through the archway because they had appeared too soon. I dare say the cold had something to do with it, their wanting to get the whole thing over with quickly.

'*Oggi vi e nato nella città di Davide un salvatore,*' announced one of the angels. '*Troveranno un bambino avvolto in fasce, che giace in una mangiatoia.*'

And indeed there was the baby, looking pink and plastic and surrounded by a halo of lights. It was the kind of baby which intones 'Mamma' when you put it to your shoulder and then dribbles down your back. *Sbrodolina*, it is called, which loosely translated is 'little puker'. They advertised them on television.

'*Andiamo fino a Betlemme,*' suggested one of the shepherds, barging the sheep into line. The faithful applauded. '*Mannaggia!*' muttered Joseph as the donkey stepped on his foot. The shepherds battled with their animals and the deacon battled with the shepherds and the heavenly choir sang, '*Gloria a Dio nel più alto dei cieli,*' and Mary looked down at the baby with a look of real love. Perhaps the doll was hers.

Finally the Three Wise Men were allowed on, bearing their gifts but without their camels, those being the one item of livestock that Avea could not supply. There was more applause. The wind tunnelled its way through the arches and alleyways of the old village and scattered straw across the setts of the piazza. Breath rose in clouds above the huddled spectators. Joseph blew his nose on his sleeve and one of the angels threw a punch at a magus and Don Anastasio stepped forward to pluck the pink plastic baby from its manger and hold it aloft for all to see. If this were untrue I would write that she puked down his sleeve, but it is true and she didn't.

'*La vergine conciperà e partorirà un figlio che sarà chiamato Emanuele, che significa Dio con noi,*' he announced.

Without a hint of self-consciousness he turned from the scene and, with the pink plastic baby held on high, climbed the steps into the breath-taking cold of the church. We followed in solemn procession. The baby was placed on the high altar in a second crib all hung with lights, just where, in more normal times, the crucifix would be. As the clock on the campanile began to sound midnight Don Anastasio turned to the congregation.

'*Nel nome del Padre e del Figlio e dello Spirito Santo.*'

'*Amen.*'

And so he began to celebrate midnight mass in the church of San Lorenzo before a plastic doll called Little Puker. Christmas had come.

The next morning we called in on the Colasanti. Compared with the Rossi they were positively international in their celebration of the feast. In their sitting room a Christmas tree stood beside the crib and there were little packages hanging from its branches, doubtless filled with tasteful trinkets from Gucci. Father Christmas had, it seemed, already been. Pia wore a red bow in her hair and gold at her throat while Lorenzo, immaculate in new hand-sewn shoes and Valentino slacks, brandished a bottle of chilled Dom Perignon. The cork came out with a bang. He tilted the bottle expertly to prevent the wine foaming out and flute-glasses clinked together as we drank to the season in a kind of English that has only ever existed in the minds of Hollywood film producers: 'Chin-chin,' everyone said.

Their younger son tugged at my sleeve to take me down to his play room and demonstrate his motor-racing set. '*Babbo natale* brought it,' he explained with a knowing smile. Doubtless he had it planned that la Befana would come in her time.

'He's so excited,' Pia explained fondly. 'It's what he always wanted.'

The track was extensive. It wound its way round the furniture like the old Nürburgring. There were pits and grandstands and crash barriers and an ambulance waiting pessimistically beside the chicane.

'Monza,' he announced. He grabbed up the control and sent one of the cars screaming round at what must have been a scale speed of about four hundred kilometres per hour. The

car left the track at a curve and rolled into a group of spectators.

'*Vincono i Ferrari*? I asked hopefully.

He shook his head sadly. '*Vincono i MacLaren.*' Then he
brightened, beckoning me over to a cupboard. 'Do you want
to see this?' He pulled a drawer open. Within lay a box full of
bangers, wicked-looking things made of red cardboard with
blue detonators stuck in one end. They were like miniature
sticks of dynamite.

'*Raudi.*' His expression was beatific. The word is pronounced exactly like the English 'rowdy', which is perhaps
appropriate enough.

'Does your mother know about them?' I asked anxiously,
responsible parenthood weighing heavily on my mind.

'Mama bought them for me,' he said. 'For *capodanno.*'
*Capodanno* is New Year's Day. He made a sharp sideways
gesture with his fist. '*Capodanno* we go boom,' he said.

# 18

*Capodanno* is a frightening event. Underlying all Italian society is a fine sense of anarchy and *capodanno* is the moment when it bursts to the surface. The word is *capo d'anno*, head of the year, but it might just as well be *capo danno*, chief damage, for if Christmas Day is the day of creation, then New

Year's Day is the day of destruction. We were invited by the Colasanti for dinner and the evening seemed mild enough, quite pleasant really, a fire blazing in their huge fireplace, red wine glinting in glasses, a table laden with provisions, all that kind of thing. But outside, in the streets of the village, kids ran like wild cats for the shadows, leaving fireworks to detonate in their wake with nerve-shattering reports. Some of the devices are even miniaturised so that you can hold them in the hand as they explode. Needless to say, the worst accidents are in Naples.

The meal was splendid. Pia did not do the cooking, of course: there was her *donna* from the village to do that. We ate home-made ravioli stuffed with *ricotta* and spinach, and drank the curiously named Est Est Est as the accompanying wine while explosions sounded off in the background.

'You know the story of Est Est Est?' Lorenzo asked, holding his glass aloft. Outside, children's voice called. His younger son looked desperately towards the door.

No, we admitted, we did not know the story. We were surely the only foreigners in Italy who did not.

'Ah.' He examined the wine thoughtfully. 'There was this German cardinal, travelling back home after the coronation of the Emperor Henry V in 1111. A date one cannot forget. The bishop's name was Fugger. You know the name, I expect? I'm afraid the Italians corrupted it to Gianni DeFuk, which I think doesn't sound very good in English.'

'Fugger's not much better.'

'Isn't it? Anyway this Fugger used to send his servant ahead during his travels to sample the local wine. Have you really not heard this? Where the wine was good this servant was to write the slogan "est bonum" on the wall. Ees good, you understand?'

'Perfectly.' Another explosion rent the air.

'*Babbo*, can I go out?' the younger son pleaded.

'Not yet. We haven't finished. Now where was I? Ah, yes. So when this servant came to the town of Montefiascone, from where this' – he sipped appreciatively – 'wine comes, he was so impressed that he wrote the word three times on the wall, thus: est est est. It is, it is, it is. Hence the name. Actually, most of the wine is very poor these days. The one you are drinking is the only one of note and it isn't made in Montefiascone at all but in the town of Bolsena. Mazziotti. Maybe we can pay a visit one day.'

I recalled the tomb-robbing expedition and I prayed not.

'*Babbo,* can I go out?' pleaded the boy.

His father ignored him. 'And the good bishop? Of course he too found the wine good, so he stayed in Montefiascone and never bothered to go home at all. In fact, as might be expected from a German, he enjoyed the wine so much that he drank himself to death.' Lorenzo looked up with satisfaction. 'Like all good Italian stories it is not only improbable but actually *true*. I will show you the man's tomb, in the church of San Flaviano. It was his servant who caused the epitaph to be written: *Hic jacet J. DeFuk, dominus meus, qui propter nimium Est Est Est mortuus est.* You understand Latin? I don't know how the English schools are.'

'I did some. *Nimium?*'

'*Un eccesso.* "Here lies Gianni de Fuk, my master, who died through an excess of Est Est Est." You amaze me. I thought everyone knew the story.'

'*Babbo,* can I go out?'

'There is the *abbacchio* still to come. *Poi zampone e cotecchino con lenticchie.* You may *not* go out.'

'But my friends . . .'

'Your friends will be out in the streets until midnight. You can wait.'

*Abbacchio* is Roman lamb; *zampone* is pig's trotter and *cotecchino* is a kind of large sausage. Both are traditionally eaten on New Year's Eve with lentils. The tradition – but this is an Italian story that is assuredly not true – is that the more lentils you manage at *capodanno* the more money you will make in the coming year. When the *donna* came in with the bowl of steaming pulses we viewed it with a certain falling of the spirits, and a sense that our personal economy was not going to do too well in the coming year.

Lorenzo looked round the table decisively. 'Now, with the meat we cannot possibly drink a wine from Lazio. There are no red Laziale wines worth the name. I have instead some Sassicaia. Do you know it?'

I didn't, then.

He nodded. 'It is not well known. Not yet. It is about to become the most celebrated Italian red. It is made with the Cabernet Sauvignon grape . . .'

'Claret?' I knew that much.

'Not a good name. Bordeaux. But this is made in the Tuscan *maremma* near Grosseto. Not the place one associates with wines of any kind, never mind great ones. The producer is the Marchese Incisa della Rochetta, whose main occupation has been racehorses. Ribot was his most famous – you have heard of Ribot? He won the Arc de Triomphe two years running in the nineteen fifties.'

'I'm not really a follower.'

Lorenzo shrugged. 'And the Marchese stumbled on to wine-making by accident. Always a winner, it seems. Now who knows what he will be remembered for? It is,' he added, raising his glass, 'rather expensive.'

In the candlelight the wine gleamed the colour of garnet. It was dark and smooth and powerful, a massive thing unlike any other Italian red I had tasted, or, I guessed, was likely to taste very often in the future.

'You must eat on behalf of your son,' Lorenzo urged, indicating the lentils on my plate. I toyed with a few forkfuls and felt my bank account shrinking beyond the point where it would be able to afford any Sassicaia. Perhaps the myth is true after all. When we had made a brave attempt at the trotters and had drunk the Sassicaia, the younger son was released from the table like a rabbit from a trap. For the adults remaining behind there were *dolci* and Vin Santo, and coffee and more

Vin Santo – there was a story about that as well, but I forget it – and then it was all but midnight. The boy had reappeared with a gaggle of children from the village and we all herded into the *piazzetta* outside. By now thunder flashes were going off all round us. It was as though urban terrorists were loose in the village; a few rockets weaved drunkenly up into the darkness and scattered sparks across the rooftops.

'Come on, *Babbo!*' Lorenzo's son yelled. 'Let's go!'

Fireworks had appeared in the father's hands, nestling alongside his lit cigarette. The kids cheered. He stopped and lined up three empty bottles of Bishop Fugger's ruin so they were ranged across the basalt setts like so many trench mortars, then popped the rockets into place as though planting cuttings.

'*Due minuti,*' someone called. The kids hopped about in excitement. '*Dai, dai!*' they urged him.

Lorenzo held his cigarette aloft. It was like an angry, anarchic eye gleaming in the darkness. The clock on the church tower began to strike midnight.

'*Ora!*' they shouted.

He took a drag on the cigarette and leant down to touch its glowing end on the tails of the beasts.

'*Forza!*'

There was an eruption of flame and one of the rockets streaked across the square, barely topping the house on the other side. Another weaved drunkenly off course and disappeared into the campanile of the church nearby. The third flew horizontally and exploded with a shower of sparks against the wall opposite.

'*Attenzione!*' someone called, but whether at the gunlayer or at anyone who might get in the firing line was not clear.

'*Forza!*' screamed the kids. And in the background, above the roar of pyrotechnics, the smashing began. I saw a bottle arch through the air and explode in fragments on the ground before something grabbed me by the shoulder and spun me round.

'*Auguri e buon anno*,' said Pia. She enveloped me with the heady scent of perfume and the feathery touch of silver fox. Over her shoulder I watched another bottle describe a gentle parabola to destruction. Elsewhere there was a splintering of wood and the concussion of more glass breaking.

'It seems mad,' I said feebly.

Pia laughed. 'Out with the old,' she said, as though that explained everything. C was standing beside the pram, protecting the baby from stray rockets. The kids were weaving round her like drunks, sparklers blazing in their hands.

'Happy New Year,' I wished her.

'If we make it that far,' she replied.

Later we walked back home through the dark and empty village. An occasional explosion sounded away in the distance as though mopping-up operations were still taking place. The streets were awash with broken glass. Outside the Palazzo Rossi a broken table lay half in the road, half across the pavement and we were forced to pick our way round it. It was as though an army had passed through, leaving wreckage and destruction in its wake. We climbed wearily up the stairs to the flat and found the landing was littered with broken glass; but there were no wounded in sight.

'We made it,' I said. New Year's Day was a holiday. We'd have to wait until the day after to read about the casualties in the newspaper. So we had begun our second full year in Italy, a new year full of contradictions.

In those days in Avea it was easy to feel cut off from the rest of the country, indeed from the rest of Europe. The *paese* and the surrounding hills enclosed one like a womb and there was something of the self-sufficiency of the subsistence farmer about life there, the sensation that, if things came to the worst, we could always barricade ourselves in and survive by what the land could produce. The fact was that it often seemed that things might indeed come to the worst, because there was an outside world beyond Avea's green hills. In it inflation raged at over 20 per cent a year, industry was crippled by disruption and dispute, and violence was rife. For these were the years of political terrorism, *gli anni di piombo*, the years of lead.

For the origins of this phenomenon you must go back to the student movement of the 1960s and a political system which allowed no effective change of government. The one created a group of people with a taste for plotting, for direct action, for the grand and often violent gesture, while the other created frustration. Frustration is a powerful factor in the life of an Italian. He feels frustration before the bureaucracy, frustration before the taxation office – over 50 per cent of Italians pay their taxes because they have no option (they are on PAYE), whereas the shopkeepers and small businesses, the doctors and the lawyers all evade tax on a massive scale – above all, the Italian feels frustration before the political class which mismanages the country, accepts no responsibility for its actions, and leads a life of privilege, graft, and comfort. It is not a pretty picture, and the fact that the frustration only boiled over amongst a small and ultimately isolated (for a while it didn't look as though that would be so) section of the community is actually remarkable.

There is another thing, rarely mentioned: the fathers and sometimes the mothers of the students of the 1960s had themselves been involved in a clandestine war. This was the partisan war against the Germans and the Fascists. It was a civil war that almost became a revolution, a clandestine war in which the forces of democracy had thrown Molotov cocktails and toted sub-machine-guns. But in that war the issues had been sufficiently stark for any number of motives to be mixed into that simple word 'democracy' and appeals to the spirit of *la Resistenza* are a commonplace of Italian political life from all parts of the political spectrum. So is it any wonder that some of the frustrated student activists of the 1960s went underground a decade later? After all, they were doing no more than their parents had done in 1944 by taking to the mountains. They were following the spirit of *la Resistenza*.

It was out of this confused and confusing background that *Le Brigate Rosse*, the Red Brigades, were born and for three or four years they were a background against which ordinary life went on. The previous March I had spent a week in the Abruzzi with a group of friends, climbing mountains which top two and a half thousand metres, walking for days at a time without ever seeing anyone but a shepherd or a farmer, descending into the valleys to *paesi* which give something of the flavour of alpine villages before the coming of tourists and skiers. In that week there had been no radio and no television and reference to events in Rome we had only understood with hindsight.

'È un macello a Roma,' the owner of a trattoria had said when we told him that we lived there. We had taken it for the normal prejudices of a countryman and had agreed with him. His words conjured up traffic jams, crowds and confusion, the penalties of city life. Rome is a mess. But *macello* can also mean massacre.

'I live in a little village,' I explained defensively. 'Outside Rome.' And he nodded in approval and got on with the business in hand which was serving *spaghetti all'Amatriciana* and *lombata di vitello*. Outside the trattoria the occasional shrouded figure stumped through the streets in wellington boots. The sky was trying to decide whether to snow. There was the acrid scent of wood-smoke on the air and the raw touch of damp. With the mountains brooding above us in the dusk, Rome seemed so far away as to be discounted. But *macello* also means massacre.

We found out three days later, riding back to the city on a public bus. The driver turned the radio on and the news broadcast was a garbled account of horror. When the coach reached the suburb of San Lorenzo we began to understand, for at the cemetery beside the basilica they had been holding the funerals. There were crowds milling around helplessly. There were *carabinieri* and *polizia* in dress uniform, soldiers' combat jackets, armoured cars, buses full of riot police, the whole paraphernalia of an impotent State.

'Kidnap,' we heard. 'They've kidnapped Moro.'

And slowly, across the gulf of half-understood language, we began to comprehend: the Christian Democrat leader Aldo Moro had been kidnapped while on his way to Parliament. All five of his escort had been gunned down without being able to react. Moro had been snatched. The whole attack had taken place in the middle of a middle-class suburb of the city and had lasted bare minutes. The kidnappers had got clean away.

It is hard to supply a British equivalent because Moro the politician was a peculiarly Italian phenomenon, the kind of man who was only really at home in the tortuous maze of Italian political life. He was the man of the 'opening to the left', the man of 'historic compromise' and 'parallel convergence'. English politics are altogether simpler. Perhaps, to put it into some kind of context, one might imagine Harold Wilson kidnapped by the IRA at nine o'clock of a weekday morning in Chelsea, but Harold Wilson being driven in convoy with an escort car and a total of five armed plain-clothes policemen on duty . . .

So we witnessed a nation paralysed with shock, like rabbits caught in the headlights of a car. We were treated to coarse-grained photographs of the victim taken in the 'People's Prison', with the Red Brigades flag as a backdrop and a copy of the previous day's newspaper in his hand. Anguished but resigned, suffused, in fact, with that terrible sense of fatalism which is part of the national psyche, his expression still haunts the Italian mind. That face knew that it was going to die.

We watched the political parties manoeuvring and offering nothing but 'no deal'. We saw the forces of law and order milling around impotently. We witnessed an appeal by the Pope himself to the 'men of the Red Brigades', pleading, so he said, on bended knees for the life of their victim. The nation caught its breath in horror at the idea, but I couldn't understand why. What else would the founder of the religion have done? On Good Friday the Pope washes the feet of a group of the faithful in Saint Peter's, in memory of Christ washing the disciples' feet before the Last Supper. When the Pope made his appeal to the Red Brigades, the cartoonist Forattini portrayed this event in the front page of *La Repubblica*. But the foot the Pope was washing was that of the Red Brigades, and it was clad in a Fascist boot.

'The Red Brigades must be run from outside Italy,' Lorenzo asserted confidently. There was a kind of cynical logic about his argument. 'The whole attack was too efficient. It couldn't have been done by Italians on their own. They'd have messed it up.' So, like so many of his countrymen, he dragged in the CIA or the KGB and had the whole thing solved: it was a foreign conspiracy. That not only explains it, but it also somehow shifts the blame.

'It is,' Lorenzo asserted, 'a communist plot.'

'But the Communist Party has taken the government line,' I argued. 'They are against the Red Brigades, they want no negotiation with them at all.'

It was an objection easily pushed aside. 'They *say* they want no negotiation. That is part of the plot.'

The problem with the conspiracy theory of history is that it is as elusive as the conspiracies it invokes. Lorenzo's argument would be repeated word for word in the Bar Rasenna by supporters of the Communist Party. All they had to do was substitute the letters CIA for KGB and the term 'Fascist' for 'Communist'. It works just as well.

'It's a plot to turn the people away from the PCI,' they argued, with some conviction. 'Just as the Party is coming into power, just as it's gaining as many votes as the *democristiani*, just as something is changing . . .'

Meanwhile, with a wailing of sirens and a scream of tyres, *gli anni di piombo* came to Avea in the shape of a *carabinieri* raid. Blue lamps sparked outside the main gate as vans and trucks drew to a halt. Men in combat jackets leaped down, brandishing sub-machine-guns. Doors slammed, orders were shouted, boots clumped across the tarmac and into the *centro storico*. The old boys in the bar looked up from their arguments and their games of *scopa*. The women grabbed their children to their sides and huddled in protective groups in the alleys to witness this intrusion of the outside world on their lives.

A *carabinieri* officer, resplendent in black and red and silver, was in charge. 'We've had a tip-off,' was all he would say. He wore leather gloves and he punched one fist decisively into the other as he waited for the outcome. The mayor was called out of the offices of the *comune* to consult with the forces of law and order. Inside the *centro storico* they were ransacking a deserted house, tramping their way through an empty church, shaking their heads about it all.

'They haven't the faintest idea what they're doing,' was the view of the customers at the bar.

The raid ended as rapidly as it had begun. The troops trotted back through the village and climbed into their transport; the officer saluted the mayor with fine parade-ground spirit. The blue lights were still flashing. The vehicles screamed away from the village just as fast as they had come and slowly the crowds dispersed, muttering. In the bar they returned to their *scopa*.

'They're clutching at straws,' Lorenzo claimed. He had, of course, found some further news: 'The story is that they've even been consulting some medium, a Dutchman or something. He's had a dream about Moro's prison being in a village outside Rome.' We all laughed. Like all good Italian stories it was not only improbable, it was actually *true*.

For weeks we lived with military roadblocks on all the roads out of the city while they searched desperately for any trace of the missing politician. Travelling to and from work one grew used to being flagged into the side and looking up into the blank O of a sub-machine-gun's muzzle.

'What have you got in the boot?' I was asked by one soldier.

By then it had been going on for over a month and had yielded nothing. His tone was hopeless.

'Nothing,' I replied.

He never even bothered to look. '*Vada, vada,*' he said, waving me on.

For forty days – a figure heavy with symbolism – no trace was found, and by the time the end came the manoeuvring amongst the political class had been such that there was no longer room left for Moro anyway. The gap created by his kidnapping had been closed up; things had been said and done which were irrevocable. The positions had all shifted. There was never any real doubt. Letters in Moro's hand came from the People's Prison begging, suggesting, pleading, arguing, but his colleagues were implacable in their adherence to the *linea dura*, the hard line. There never was any real doubt.

So the wheels of fate ground inexorably round and finally spat out his crumpled and unshaven body into the boot of a Renault 4. They had parked the car in a side street midway between the headquarters of the Christian Democrats and the headquarters of the Communists, in daylight, in the middle of the week. It was the ultimate mark of contempt. Moro had been forty-four days in the 'People's Prison' and no one had lifted a finger to help him. The Italian nation drew in its breath in horror.

A week later, in communal elections the Communist Party's vote slid dramatically. 'There you are,' the experts in the Bar Rasenna said. 'We told you so.'

The Party's vote continued to slide for the next decade . . . and now there is no Party. Nothing will convince the experts in the Bar Rasenna that they were not right, just as nothing will convince Lorenzo that he is not right: 'The Russians were getting desperate. They saw the country in chaos and the Communist Party not taking its opportunity. They wanted to give things a push.'

When the end of the terrorist groups came three years later it was with dramatic suddenness. The *Brigate Rosse* had finally stepped outside the purely national scene by kidnapping an American army general, James Dozier. After being held prisoner for forty-two days in a flat in Padua, he was liberated by Italian special forces. It was a brilliant operation. No one was killed and all the general's captors were arrested.

I could imagine Lorenzo's wry smile. 'It couldn't have been done by the Italians,' he would have said. 'It was too efficient. Italians would have made a mess of it. It must have been the CIA.'

# 19

Whatever the political upheavals of the country, in spring, on Easter Monday to be precise, the *festa della Madonna del Melagrano* was held in the valley below the sanctuary. This was an event that put mere temporal politics in perspective. We went down with Pippo and Grazia and discovered the whole village encamped on the pasture beside the stream. There were groups cooking on barbecues, people boiling water for pasta, Giuseppina selling her *porchetta*, stalls selling food and wine. The voices and laughter rose in volume, the stalls blared out their music, the village band shrieked and blasted. For all the stories about appearances of the Madonna beneath a pomegranate tree, it is difficult to believe that this bacchanalian celebration is in any way a Christian festival – as Lorenzo observed, it has all the signs of Dionysiac rite tamed by time and the grave frown of the Papacy. At any moment one expected maenads to come raging out of the woods with some wretched victim in their hands, and Pippo was surely a satyr, tipping a libation to the gods as he stumbled over a tree root, eyeing the women as though they might be bacchantes, tearing animals limb from limb and stuffing the pieces in his mouth. The feast raged around him and for a moment he was some mad little focus of it all.

'*Er duca! Er duca!*' they called and he raised his glass on high and tripped backwards into the bushes.

One of the chief features of the *festa* is the greasy pole.

'*L'albero della cuccagna!*' Pippo said, pointing to it. 'When I was young' – he gestured with his cupped hand, that sign of wonder and plenty – 'first to the top, I'd be. First to the top!'

The greasy pole stood erect in the midst of the chaos. It had the dimensions of a telegraph pole but with a cartwheel set horizontally at the top. From the rim of the wheel hung a fringe of salamis and hams. The pole itself was daubed with grease and the young bloods of the village were even now grappling with the thing, struggling a few feet off the ground and slithering down again, to jeers and laughter. When finally one of them arrived at the summit he would be able to grab at one of the sausages and bring his trophy to the ground.

'First to the top, I used to be!'

'Go on, Pippo, have a go now.'

He grinned and rolled his eyes.

'Bah,' said Grazia. 'He'd have a heart attack.'

Lorenzo was there with Pia, of course, for even the grandees of the village take part in the *festa*. They had ridden over from the stables and their horses cropped grass at the edge of the field. Both of them greeted the Rossi warmly, declining the offer of pieces of chicken with apparent reluctance. 'But a glass of wine, perhaps,' Lorenzo suggested by way of compromise. Pippo poured him some before returning to his task of dismembering a second roast chicken.

Lorenzo seemed to find the sight amusing. '*Sparagmos*,' he said. 'Do you know the word?'

I didn't.

'It was a Greek word for tearing or' – he gestured – 'ripping apart, used for the particular Dionysiac rite when animals were caught by the bacchantes.' The racket of the *festa* raged round him as he sipped the cloudy wine. Grazia was cutting slices of bread, holding the loaf in her arms like a baby, hacking the knife towards her. Pippo was indulging in his own personal *sparagmos* with a chicken leg.

'In a kind of divine ecstasy they would tear the animals limb from limb and eat the flesh raw,' Lorenzo explained blandly. '*Sparagmos* is the same word as the Latin verb *spargo*, "to scatter", but also "to divide" or "tear in pieces", which has become the Italian *spargere*, also "to scatter" but no longer to

213

tear apart, unless a trace remains in the sense of *spargere il sangue*, "to shed blood". Thus, you see, the word, one of the most potent of the classical age, has come down to us emasculated by time but still containing a hint of its ecstatic past. Just like this *festa*.'

'You think this was a Dionysiac feast?'

'Who could doubt it? For example Dionysus fathered Priapus by Aphrodite – do you know Priapus?'

'By reputation,' I said.

'Well a large *fallo* – you understand the word?'

I did. So did Pia. She smiled.

'A large *fallo* was a central part of the Dionysia.' Lorenzo pointed to the greasy pole. A crowd seethed round the base. Above their heads a youth had struggled two-thirds of the way to the top. He was grappling desperately just to stay where he was. 'It is difficult not to draw parallels,' Lorenzo said with a faint smile. The mob jeered and hooted as the youth slid back down. 'Of course, you can make almost any connection you like. For example Dionysus was the son of Zeus, King of the gods. On Hera's orders –' He looked at me with eyebrows raised.

'Zeus's wife. I know that much.'

'On Hera's orders the Titans killed the child. That is one of the traditions anyway. And his grandmother Rhea, the mother of Zeus, later brought him back to life.'

'A god of death and resurrection?'

'Precisely. But the point I was going to make is this: when the Titans tore him to pieces his blood fell on the ground, and where it fell a pomegranate tree grew. Maybe Rhea, equated with Cybele the Great Mother of the Gods who was one of the most popular goddesses in Rome, maybe Rhea is the real Madonna del Melagrano. How do you like that?'

'Magnificent.'

'Convincing?'

'As convincing as appearances of the Madonna to a shepherd.'

Lorenzo winced. 'Just because of one explanation you must not reject another. I feel that all things are possible, all explanations for what is a mystery may exist side by side.'

I always found it hard to imagine him making plastic bathroom fittings. As he spoke, the next attempt was being made on the greasy pole. This time the boy got up to the top. There was a cheer as he grabbed one of the spokes of the wheel and reached out for a salami, a climactic roar as he snatched the thing from its thread and tossed it to someone in the crowd below.

'Now we will leave you to enjoy your lunch,' Lorenzo said. 'Thank you for the wine.'

'*Dottore, signora, arrivederci*!' Pippo exclaimed through a mouthful of bread. Lorenzo took Pia's arm and led her away. We settled into the more sacrificial aspects of the bacchanalia.

In the spirit which Lorenzo advocated, of making any connection you like, I offer my own observation: the god himself, Dionysus or Bacchus as you please, is usually portrayed bearing a *thyrsus*. This peculiar symbol is also carried by his followers. It is a rod topped with what is usually described as a pine cone; but it often looks just like a pomegranate.

A week later we went down to Naples for the wedding of Gennaro. Grazia's family come from near Torre del Greco, a scruffy suburb of ferroconcrete and peeling plaster lying in the narrow plain between the bay and the slopes of Mount Vesuvius. Torre del Greco is a town that is trapped. It is trapped between the railway and the *autostrada*, between the volcano and the sea, between the threat of eruption and earthquake. But above all Torre del Greco is trapped by the Camorra.

The Camorra is the Neapolitan version of the Mafia. Like the Mafia itself it is more a criminal way of life rather than a specific organisation, a spirit of place, a creed – a theocracy, if you like, with a recognised clergy but no particular primate. Torre del Greco is one of its centres. Coming down from the north, with your car brandishing Rome numberplates, you feel that you are intruding on a world governed by an occult power. This is the *Mezzogiorno*, that blighted area of Italy which drags the north down like a millstone hanging from its neck. Like the Midi of France or Nofsinhar of C's own language, the name *Mezzogiorno*, literally 'midday', has come to signify the direction in which the sun stands at its zenith – the south; but in Italian the word carries with it a much greater semantic burden than a mere quarter of the compass: *Mezzogiorno* includes corruption, official indifference, systematic waste, violence. It includes ruin and poverty and hopelessness. It includes Camorra, Mafia, and *'ndrangheta*. It includes the agony of modern Italy, but it also includes a part, a large part, of its soul. You cannot have the soul without the agony. It is another of the paradoxes of the country. Whatever the smug burghers of *alto Italia* may think, Italy cannot do without the *Mezzogiorno*.

'Where did you park your car?' Pippo asked when he met us at the entrance to the church.

'Just round the corner. Near yours.'

He nodded approval. It seemed that there it would be protected. Together we went into the church. It was a hideous building of the last century, heavy with plasterwork and gilt. The pews were decked out for the ceremony in yards of lime-green tulle. At the head of the chancel steps the altar was a confection of pink marble.

'*Bello, no?*' Pippo asked.

'*Bello,*' we agreed.

Before the altar were two chairs and two prie-dieus, also swathed in lime green, where Gennaro waited with his two witnesses. He smiled nervously when he saw us.

'Looks lime green himself,' I whispered to C.

The priest was arguing with a couple of photographers about where their cables should or should not go. The photographers gave the impression that the ceremony was being staged solely for their benefit. The priest shook his head frequently, as though to disabuse them of this idea. Finally he urged them away to the sides, glanced pointedly at his watch and went over to whisper something to Gennaro. Neither looked very happy.

'The bride's late,' C whispered.

'Of course, this isn't the actual church of Grazia's *paese*,' Pippo was explaining blithely. 'They couldn't hold the wedding there.'

'No? Why not?'

He lowered his voice and leant towards us. 'Her elder brother. He was gunned down on the steps. It would have been too upsetting.'

'Murdered?' I asked, convinced that I must have misunderstood.

'*Ammazzato*,' agreed Pippo. 'By his brother-in-law.'

'By his *brother-in-law*?'

Pippo nodded, making a face which suggested both horror and faint amusement. 'His wife's brother. Imagine.'

'And what happened to him?'

'He's inside. Twenty-five years. And when he comes out . . .'

'Yes?'

'His sister will kill him.'

A voice boomed over the loudspeaker system. 'I've waited ten minutes and I'm not going to wait any longer.' We looked up. The priest was now standing before the altar with a microphone in his hand. 'People must have respect for the Church and arrive on time. I am going to begin the mass.' He went behind the altar and placed the microphone on its stand. The sound boomed round the church like a clap of thunder. The priest raised his arms in salutation. 'Brothers and sisters, we are gathered together today to sanctify the marriage before God and this congregation of . . .' he paused and leafed through some pages for the names . . . 'Gennaro and Maria Annunziata.'

But one half of the undertaking was conspicuous only by an empty pile of green tulle. Gennaro glanced over his shoulder towards the door.

'That priest had better watch it,' I whispered to C, 'otherwise they'll get him on the steps of the church and then it'll be too upsetting for them to come here as well.'

'There she is.' Pippo was pointing surreptitiously to a pew in front of us where, amongst women dressed for a wedding, two women stood dressed for a funeral. 'That's the sister, beside Grazia's mother. If the sister doesn't get him, then Grazia's mother will.'

'Please will people not talk during the service,' the priest called over the speakers. 'Show some respect for the house of God.'

Pippo started guiltily.

'*Nel nome del Padre e del Figlio e dello Spirito Santo,*' the priest boomed.

'*Amen,*' said the congregation.

'*Amen,*' agreed Pippo.

The bride arrived during the Gloria. Tight-lipped, the priest paused and beckoned her forward from the doors. As she moved, a photographer's assistant leapt into the aisle with a lamp held aloft. There was a click and a buzz and the whole church was flooded with dazzling light, an unearthly light as of angels and archangels, as of thrones, dominions and powers.

'Afterwards!' shouted the priest, waving his hands frantically. 'This is a holy mass not a television studio. You may take photographs like that afterwards!'

Afterwards Pippo would have nothing to do with it. 'Her mother wouldn't want me in the photos anyway,' he said. 'She hates me. Come outside and I'll introduce you to some friends.'

So we left C behind with Grazia and the baby and went out into the daylight. At the foot of the steps more guests were waiting, those who had had no truck with the religious part of the wedding. Two of them were Pippo's friends. 'Business colleagues,' he qualified it. They were heavy-faced, middle-aged men poured into close-cut suits. Their chests bulged, their armpits bulged, their faces bulged.

'*Piacere*,' they said, holding out massive hands. One of them bore a long scar down one cheek. 'English?'

'English,' I agreed. I'd have agreed if they'd suggested Eskimo. With Pippo they didn't shake hands in the normal manner, but squeezed right hand with left, almost as one might take a child's. There was something curiously solicitous about their manner, as if they were worried that you might be afraid of them. One of them had some American-slanted English.

'You like it here? You like Torre del Greco?'

'It's very interesting.'

'And the Bay? What you think of the Bay, then?'

'Beautiful.' Beyond the nearby buildings the bay lay all before us, from the Sorrento Peninsula on the left where the sirens sang, and Capri where everybody else sang including Gracie Fields, to Ischia lying in the haze of distance on the right. In the middle of it all there was the grey shape of an aircraft carrier lying at anchor.

'There are two bays in the whole world. San Francisco' –

he was careful to soften the first 'c' in the American fashion: San Fransisco – 'and *il golfo di Napoli*.'

'You know San Francisco?'

'I bin there. You?'

'Never.'

He nodded, as though from the start he had expected the sophisticated foreigner to let him down. 'You know what they say, the Americans?'

'What do they say?'

'See Naples and die.' He smiled. His eyes were like glass. 'That's what they say.'

I was rescued by the appearance of the bride and groom at the head of the steps.

'*Viva la sposa!*' someone called. The cry was taken up – '*Evviva gli sposi! Evviva gli sposi!*' Rice showered through the air and scattered like shrapnel across the steps. Gennaro grinned round at the crowd as though amazed to find that anyone had actually bothered to come.

'*Viva Gennaro! Viva Nunzia!*'

C had appeared from a side door with the pram. We stood in the crowd while the couple came down to ground level. The bridal car had drawn up to the bottom of the steps like a barge at a quay. It was a long, white Cadillac with fins and chrome teeth and a circlet of fairy lights round the roof and an interior of red plastic.

'You follow us in your car,' Pippo called. 'First we go to the village, then we go on to the reception. You follow us.'

His two associates were strolling away from the church towards their own vehicle. They moved smoothly, as though the pavement were oiled. Even with its eyes on the departing Cadillac, the crowd still parted to let them through.

We picked up Pippo's Alfa on the edge of the church square. A policeman held up the traffic for a moment and we shot away on to the main road in a haze of exhaust fumes and tyre smoke.

'Be careful!' C pleaded.

'If we lose them we've lost everything. I've no idea where we're going.'

'I think it might be the other way round,' she said quietly. 'If we keep up with them we might actually lose everything.'

We careered through the edge of Torre del Greco, roared under a flyover, then climbed a steep ramp on to the *auto-strada*. The slopes of Vesuvius rose up to the left: on the right the Neapolitan littoral slid past, the flat roofs, the ferrocon-crete blocks, the flat, blue water with the aircraft carrier in the distance. Ahead of us Pippo's Alfa winked its brake lights. We slid up behind it and found ourselves part of an escort. Beyond the Alfa and a dozen other cars cruised the bridal carriage with its fairy lights winking. Horns blasted from time to time as though to keep the devils away from the auspicious occasion. At the next exit the whole line of cars slid off the motorway and down into the cement once more. A sign pointed left to Vesuvio, another one right to Pompeii, and shortly we arrived at the village from where Grazia's family actually came.

San Giusto Vesuviano is a small and undistinguished place on the edge of the plain. It is dominated by the slanting black shadow of the volcano, by the threat of earthquake and eruption. There are no old buildings and there are no tall buildings. A road sign advertised Lacryma Cristi wine, but one felt that in this region it was not only Christ who was crying.

The procession of cars slowed down as the houses came nearer. There were people waiting on the pavements, crowds of people lined up as though expecting a royal visit. The car at the head of the procession began to blast its horn and all the cars took up the sound, blaring and shrieking like a Neapolitan traffic jam. As we passed, the people threw up their arms as though in some kind of hieratic salute and a blizzard of colour floated down all over the cars. At first I thought it was the paper confetti of English weddings, but the soft, pastel flakes falling across our windscreen were rose petals. We drove through the streets of Grazia's village, past the church where they couldn't hold the wedding because her brother had been gunned down on the steps, past the large concrete villa which was apparently the family home, through the wreckage of earthquake and organised crime, and all the time we drove through a cloud of falling rose petals.

The reception was held far away, at one of those huge restaurants which advertise *salone per banchetti*, banqueting room, almost as a warning to the casual customer: here is a factory dedicated to the serving of hundreds at a time! Intimate diners beware! That lunchtime three hundred sat down to eat . . .

It bears some consideration, this. As with Vesuvius you need to stand back to get it in perspective: the meal began at one o'clock, give or take a bride and groom who were having their formal photos taken amongst the ruins of Pompeii, and we finally left at six-thirty after the cutting of the cake. The meal had still not ended. The band – *I Nuovi Partenopei*, all glitter and electronics – was playing still and looked set for the night. You didn't just go to the reception to eat a meal and wish the happy couple well; you camped at your table for half a day and went home with enough food to feed a family into the next week.

We sat with Pippo and Grazia. We ate, we danced, we ate again. We went up to the high table to be presented to Grazia's mother, a small, fierce woman dressed in black who received the *baciamano*, the hand-kissing, from the guests in the manner of a feudal chief, a Boudicca, perhaps, accepting the homage of her vassals. We returned to the table to more food. We danced some more. Long ago we had lost the baby to a flock of beribboned girls who cooed over him and rushed him off to demonstrate the possibilities to the blushing Nunzia. We ate some more.

'*Viva la sposa!*' someone cried.

'*Viva la sposa!*' the guests replied, sinking another toast.

Nunzia smiled shyly, never before the subject of such attention, never since. Defeated, we pushed the fifth dish – a whole mullet the size of a salmon – aside.

'*Piano, piano,*' Pippo advised. He spoke from experience. The Lacryma Cristi flowed, undistinguished, unobjectionable, alcoholic. A waiter distributed sheets of paper from a roll precisely so that the guests could wrap excess food and take it home.

'There they are.' Pippo leaned back in his chair and waved at a nearby table. I turned to see our erstwhile friends from the church steps sitting with another four companions of similar stamp. They raised their hands. I waved cheerily back at them.

'Imagine how many years that table has done,' Pippo said. 'Eh?'

'Imagine,' he repeated. He was smiling and bobbing at them. 'Imagine.' He wasn't speaking rhetorically. I was meant to do just that.

'Fifteen?' I hazarded.

'Keep your voice down or they'll realise we're talking about them,' he cautioned. 'Fifty-five.'

'*Fifty-five*? That's an average of nine years each.'

'One of them has never been convicted.'

I revised my mathematics upwards.

'And that one over there.' He indicated an innocuous little fellow at another table, a small mouse-like man hedged about with raucous females. 'Twenty-five. Twenty with good behaviour.'

'But he looks only about thirty.'

'Thirty-five. He's just come out.'

'He was fifteen?'

Pippo nodded. 'Fifteen. His cousin.'

'He killed his cousin?'

'Blew his head off with a *lupara*.' The *lupara* is a shorn-off shotgun, much loved in the *Mezzogiorno*. 'They had a row in a bar, you see, and this cousin slapped him about a bit. In front of friends. So that fellow went home, took his father's gun, went back to the bar and shot his cousin.'

'Just like that.'

'Just like that.'

'In the bar.'

Pippo held his hands out. 'Obvious. The audience was important. Without the audience . . .'

The sixth dish was a grilled baby chicken *alla diavola*, followed mercifully by a water ice. The band played a version of '*O Sole Mio*' that sounded like Little Tony, and then the singer lowered her voice and clutched the microphone to her mouth and sang a true Neapolitan song, '*Santa Lucia Luntana*'. She was bright and flashy, but her voice had that ragged edge of pain which is so much part of the city. The noise of the party died away over the *pollo alla diavola*.

> *Santa Lucia,*
> *Luntano'a te*
> *Quanta malicunia!*

The words were slurred with sadness, husky with that resource which is never lacking in the city, sentimentality. Was this the song the sirens sang? Maybe she was Parthenope, the siren whose body was washed up on the shore where Naples now stands.

> *Se gira'o munno sano,*
> *se va a cercà furtuna . . .*
> *ma, quanno sponta'a luna,*
> *luntano'a Napule nun se po'stà!*

You might travel the whole world, you might go in search of fortune, but when the moon rises no one can stay far from Naples. Banal enough maybe. But the girl finished by singing just two words from the refrain into a total silence: *quanta malicunia!* how much melancholy! In Italian, as in Neapolitan, the word has gained something from its echoes of *male* – evil, pain, suffering, whatever you like. As the sound died away there was that moment's stillness, then the guests were cheering and stamping and standing to raise their glasses.

Pippo had tears in his eyes. '*Che bona,*' he said.

Thus purged by emotion the guests moved on to the seventh dish.

We left after Nunzia and Gennaro had cut the cake and circulated round the room bringing pieces to the guests, Gennaro serving the women, Nunzia the men.

'*Viva San Gennaro!*' shouted Pippo.

The crowd cheered with delight. San Gennaro is the patron saint of Naples. Two phials of his blood are kept in a chapel in the Duomo and are brought out on certain significant days during the year. Amidst much cursing and many imprecations this stuff is expected to liquify. If it fails, bad luck is bound to follow. The change or no of San Gennaro's blood frequently makes the main news broadcast on television and the sophisticated newsreaders are always uncertain how to pitch the story. It would never do to joke about it, for to the chief city of the *Mezzogiorno* San Gennaro matters – and so does the state of his blood. The tone they normally manage is that of an unconfirmed report, possibly somewhat exaggerated but nevertheless worthy of cautious consideration.

'*Viva San Gennaro!*' the guests called, and Gennaro bobbed and grinned as though they were calling for his own canonisation.

So we bade Gennaro and Nunzia goodbye. '*Mi biac' i stranieri,*' he assured us. He even gave C a kiss. Nunzia looked faintly confused. She probably had no idea who we were, but, just like San Gennaro's blood liquifying, having foreigners to your wedding brings good luck.

Somehow we retrieved the baby from the girls, and our package of fish from our table, and a little present from the happy couple along with the traditional bag of *confetti*, sugared almonds. Outside, it was already dusk and we had the *autostrada* back to Rome to face. In the restaurant the band had struck up *'Torna a Surriento'*, but the girl didn't sound like Little Tony.

'Look.' I pointed up into the sky. High above us the summit of Vesuvius was touched orange by the sun. 'It looks as though it's going to erupt.'

It hasn't; not yet.

# 20

One day Margaret, the wife of the medical student from Bergamo, had knocked on the door to the flat in great excitement.

'Have you seen this new law?'

C looked round from dealing with the baby. 'Law?'

'Rent control. I've been talking to the people in the office downstairs and they've explained it to me. It applies to us. We can calculate how much we should pay Pippo. *Equo canone*, it's called. It's just come out.'

C's expression was glum. 'And we'll have to pay more?'

'We'll have to pay less! We only have to measure the apartments and fill in a form. It's easy. From that you calculate the rent. The office has got the forms.'

'And who says it'll be less?'

'I did a rough estimate. Ours will come down by a third, I reckon.' For Margaret and Ugo, more than for most, every little counted.

'And then what do we do?'

Her face fell. 'And then we have to confront Pippo with it.' She paused. Nothing more needed to be said, really, but she said it. 'He'll go mad.'

There was a silence. Footsteps clipped across the ceiling. Pippo? There was a television blaring along the corridor, the usual gunfight at the OK Corral. Both Margaret and C contemplated the vision of Pippo in a rage.

'But it's the law?' C asked.

Margaret shrugged. *'Equo Canone*. It means "fair rent". Look, I've got a form here.' She rooted around in her bag and produced an official document. 'You just fill in the details in the various boxes – size of rooms, type of rooms, number of bathrooms, size of balconies, all that kind of thing . . . There's even a box here for heating.'

'And then you show it to Pippo.'

'And then you show it to Pippo.' She pointed. 'There's a box for the landlord's signature, and one for the tenant's.'

C glanced at the thing and shrugged. 'But surely all this refers to registered contracts. Ours aren't.' By law, another of those Italian laws consigned to the scrap-heap of evasion, all rental contracts had to be legally registered. To protect the tenants, was the claim; to check on landlords' tax returns was the fact.

'No, ours aren't registered.' Margaret's expression was resigned. 'Maybe that's the problem. Maybe we can't do anything about it after all. It was just a hope.'

'Can I borrow the form?' C asked. 'Just to have a look.'

Margaret dug into her bag again. 'I got one for you as well,' she admitted sheepishly.

I came home that afternoon to find C on her knees with a tape measure.

'What on earth are you up to?'

'What does it look like? I'm measuring the flat.'

'Checking to see if Pippo has finished it?'

She didn't even smile. 'Take this down. There's a piece of paper on the table. Twelve nine.'

'Twelve nine what? What on earth are you up to?'

'I'm measuring the flat to see how big it is, for that new law. The form's on the table. We might be able to reduce our rent. Now take the figure down.'

I picked up the end of the tape measure. 'Why are you measuring it in feet and inches?'

'Because I'm using my sewing tape.' There is a touch of the Irish about the Maltese.

*

228

The road to bad legislation is paved with good intentions. *Equo Canone* was one such. The idea – which is wonderful, liberal, equitable – is that you can define the rental value of a property according to a universal formula, and that such a value will be enforceable in law. Furthermore you can build into the formula a multiplier which will be reviewed each year and which will be increased by a factor related to the rate of inflation. Obvious. No argument. Everybody happy, tenant and landlord alike.

Of course the result, painfully obvious from the start, was almost completely the opposite of what was intended. What was intended was that the acute housing shortage would be solved by encouraging landlords to put their empty properties on to the market. What happened was that those few properties on the rental market immediately disappeared, because the crucial thing in the whole law was how much the landlord would actually get. All detail was irrelevant in the face of that single fact. What would the rent actually be? The fact was that, in a country with a shortage of housing, under the new law the landlord would not get a market price.

So *Equo Canone* was implemented and the rental market dried up completely and the only beneficiaries were people like us who already had somewhere to live. We could be doing what C now did, poring over the form which Margaret had supplied, writing figures (inches carefully multiplied by 2.54) into boxes, then feeding them into little formulae and adding the bits up and finally multiplying the whole figure by the index for that year and coming up with the new rent. If it was higher than what you were paying, presumably you kept quiet and hoped the landlord hadn't been reading the newspapers; if it was lower, you stumped upstairs to his flat and hammered on the door.

'Law?' said Pippo, glancing nervously over his shoulder. 'What law?'

C explained. She put the completed form in front of him. He peered at it desperately, scratching at his chin with grimy

229

fingers. Our rent had been 130,000 lire a month – about sixty pounds. Under the *Equo Canone* law it would be 93,000 lire. One hundred and thirty thousand wasn't a bad rent, in fact – it was the lack of heating that brought it down. We felt there was a certain justice in that.

'I don't know anything about a law.'

'But it's there all right. And according to it we should be paying ninety-three thousand lire a month. Because there isn't any heating.'

The voice that exploded from his diminutive frame was remarkable for its ferocity. 'Ninety-three thousand? *Porca Madonna!*' He glared at us like a bull in a pen.

'If the heating had been installed, things would have been different,' C said mildly. 'But without heating . . .'

'*Vaffanculo!*' he yelled.

'It's better to be well-mannered about it.'

Pippo picked the paper up and with a fine sense of drama – he might have been Scarpia in the second act of *Tosca* – crumpled it in one pudgy hand and threw it away. 'There, that's what I think of your *fottuta* law!'

'But it's *your* law as well. And that's only a copy. Anyway, we had it checked by the office below and they say we've done it right –'

'The office below? *Traditori! Bastardi!* You can stuff your ninety-three thousand!'

'And they told me that if the landlord refuses to accept the new rent, then the tenant is to open a bank account in his name and pay the rent into that.'

So our rent came down. Down too came Margaret and Ugo's.

'It's all your fault!' Pippo yelled at C. 'You put her up to it.'

In vain did C protest.

'Margarita is too good to do anything like that,' he insisted. 'Too good. It's you! You, you ungrateful foreigners.' It was the first and only time we were ever referred to as foreigners in a derogatory sense. To Pippo it seemed to be the ultimate insult, ranking far above his usual blasphemies. '*Stranieri ingrati!*' The sound echoed down the stairwell at our departing backs.

Was it that row which first spurred us to look for somewhere else to live? Not that alone, but there was no doubt that relations were different from then on. Pippo was that bit less admiring of C; Grazia, while never losing her devotion to the baby, was a shade cooler. But there were other things far beyond our control, the shifts of history, those small changes in the balance of society that appear trivial at the time but in retrospect loom large: Avea was being invaded.

Italy has always been plagued by invasion. The peninsula is both a corridor and a goal in itself, so it has suffered both ways – either trampled on by armies passing through, or ransacked by invaders desperately trying to acquire treasures in the mistaken hope that thereby they will acquire culture. When the Gauls rampaged down as far as Rome in the fourth century BC they were in pursuit of riches; when the Allies slogged their way up from Salerno during the last war they were hoping to use the country as a corridor, a way into the soft underbelly of the Axis powers. Vandals, Goths, Lombards, French, Spanish, Germans, they have all been here as invaders at some time or other. One of the reasons the foreigner is accepted so readily is that he is so familiar.

Yet Avea seems to have been passed by these incursions. Certainly there is the war memorial in the Piazza Garibaldi, but it records no disaster within the village itself. The village names are all there – Buonarotti, Colasanti, Rossi and others – but the victims died far away in Friuli during the First World War, or in Russia and North Africa during the Second. We know of no invasion by the revolutionary French or the Imperials of Charles V on their way to sack Rome, no raid by the Saracens, no battle between Ghibelline and Guelf, no scrap between Orsini and Colonna. If Hannibal's Carthaginians came by, we have no record of it (although they did sack the shrine of Lucas Feronia not far away), and how the ancient Romans finally wrested the place from the Etruscans we have no means of telling. By and large, tucked away from the main roads, hidden amongst its hills and gorges, Avea has always seemed immune from rape and pillage.

But this final invasion was an insidious one which could not be avoided by any of the strategies which had worked in the past. The twentieth century, almost over elsewhere, could not be kept out. '*Sono porchi, questi Romani*.' But also: '*sono ricchi*.' Not far away they were building the *autostrada*. Nearby they were building a luxury housing estate with swimming pool and tennis courts, and a small shopping centre which would boast fashion shops and an *erborista* and an *enoteca* selling prestigious vintages from Tuscany and Piemonte . . . even Sassicaia.

'You want to buy something in the old village,' Lorenzo advised us. 'This place is going to boom.'

We groaned.

'I'll help you sort things out, don't you worry. You can pick something up cheap – say, fifteen million – spend the same amount on it again and end up with a property worth fifty, sixty million. Overnight profit of almost one hundred per cent.'

This was more like the manufacturer of bathroom fittings. He exuded all the confidence of someone who had done exactly what he boasted, but also the confidence of someone who had done it with money to spare. We looked through our savings and calculated the cost of mortgages . . . and wondered.

'Come and see,' he told us one day. 'I've found just the place for you.'

We met him in the old village, down by the abandoned church. He had a confident smile on his face and an ancient key in his hand. Pinned to the wall just above his head was a card saying *VENDESI* – For Sale.

'Down here. It's perfect.' He pointed into an alleyway of

Stygian gloom. 'It's a bit dark but you'll be able to do something about that with a bit of imagination. Come on.'

Before plunging into the darkness he put his hand up, snatched the For Sale notice from the wall and tossed it away into the shadows. 'There,' he said. 'It's yours.'

Groping my way after him, I couldn't help thinking that things weren't as simple as that. We waited as the ancient key ground round in the lock to open an equally ancient and almost invisible door, then tiptoed into blackness and the sour scent of damp.

'No lights, I'm afraid,' said Lorenzo's voice. C stumbled against something and gave out a little cry. 'The stairs are over here.'

We blundered around for a bit before a further door opened up above our heads and pale light filtered down into the stairwell. Lorenzo was standing at the head of the stairs. 'Come on up.' We climbed up and peered through a second door. Before us, lit from a dusty skylight, lay an expansive loft. The smell of damp had been left below to be replaced by the smell of decay. I thought of dry rot and deathwatch beetle.

'What about that, then?' Lorenzo said with pride. 'Isn't that fantastic?'

We looked. To us it was just a loft. To Lorenzo it was a modernistic palace. He clambered over beams, tripped over a loose plank, ducked under the joists, all the time waving his arms around like a conductor getting the very best out of his orchestra. 'You open the roof over there – *terrazzo*, roof garden, whatever you want. Then you divide here to create a bedroom. And all this will be the living space – open plan, of course, with light from the terrace and skylights as well. Here would be the bathroom – there's no water at the moment but that's no problem – and over there the kitchen. If I were you I'd have it open plan with the living room, but that'd be your choice. Look at these beams. Chestnut. Must be four, five hundred years old, and perfect condition. She wants fifteen million and I reckon we can beat her down to ten. What d'you say?'

We looked. I saw only a dusty expanse of planking and the roof angling down towards the floor. It was Lorenzo who had the imagination.

'Of course, I can help you with the restoration, the builders, everything. I know reliable people. What d'you think?'

What did we think? We thought, I suppose, of the risk. We thought of the agonies of obtaining planning permission, or of ignoring it and going ahead anyway, which is the Italian method. You build what you please and shrug off all attempts to stop you and you wait until the next *condono*, amnesty, when you just confess your sins and pay a derisory sum and all becomes legal. I wonder whether it is a system the government has learnt from the Church. An Our Father and a Hail Mary for blasphemy. A decade of the rosary for theft.

'We don't have much money,' we said feebly. 'It'd be a risk.'

'No risk at all. Ten million for the place, another fifteen, say, twenty for the restructuring – you could even put in a floor over there and create a whole second level. And what have you got at the end?' He was in the mood for answering his own questions. It has always seemed to me a particularly unfair form of discussion. 'Something worth sixty, seventy million – heaven knows. You can't afford not to.'

'We'll think about it,' we said.

'Think fast,' he warned. 'Things like this are starting to go like hot cakes.' He didn't say 'hot cakes'. He actually said *vanno a ruba*. They go like robbery. It is a curiously ambivalent saying.

Was it really on that occasion, when we left the old village after meeting with Lorenzo, that we saw the two men posting funeral notices? Even across a few years memory can be deceptive. It was then, or about then, while walking through the ancient gate of the village, past the Bar Rasenna and the tobacco shop beneath the arch. We paused to look. The notice

was edged in heavy black and bore the image of the Sacred Heart of Jesus at the top.

OGGI IL 24 MAGGIO
È DECEDUTO IN AVEA
## ORESTE BUONAROTTI
DI SESSANTA NOVE ANNI

*Ne danno il triste annuncio la moglie, i figli
il genero, la nuora e i parenti tutti.*

I felt a small shiver of disquiet, the sensation that something had just shifted in the calm fabric of the village.

'Is that Oreste?' C asked. 'But he's much older. Surely.' She turned to the men sticking up the posters. 'It's not the man who sells garlic, is it?'

They looked at one another. 'Garlic?'

'We buy garlic from him. He sells nuts as well. In the piazza.'

They nodded. 'Nuts, yes. That's the one, the one who sells nuts.' Sells, sold, the tense always lets you down. Oreste the garlic man, the prisoner of war, the man who had survived nine Russian winters and his own wine and still smiled, Oreste was dead. The funeral – for you bury people quickly in that part of the world – was the next day.

A simple man in life, in death Oreste was enthroned: his coffin stood at the head of the nave atop a black-shrouded catafalque. There were candles posted at all four corners, their flames glimmering unsteadily in the draught. All manner of people had crowded into the pews around it, from the *sindaco* to the meanest *contadino*, so even though we got to the church early it was already full. The sound of suppressed weeping filled the dark corners of the place like water trickling into a deep, underground cistern. Before taking their places newcomers went up to touch the black drapery and mutter a prayer, like the faithful with a relic or a statue of a saint. Renzo the village simpleton stood before the coffin like a sentinel, holding the processional cross and talking quietly to it. Perhaps he was delivering a commentary to the man for whom all this was intended, the man with the awful bowed legs and the gap-toothed grin. Up at the altar the deacon, holier than any saint, watched him carefully as though waiting for the moment to spring.

'Just as in Adam all men die, so in Christ all will be made alive, alleluia.'

Don Anastasio, vested in purple, as splendid as any Roman

emperor, stood in front of his parishioners. Before him were Lucia, and Giuseppina and her husband, and all the other relatives. We, of course, were merely figures at the back craning to see.

The ritual was a curious mixture of the practised and the impromptu, the dramatic and the farcical. Swinging the thurible, Don Anastasio moved round the coffin. The church was silent, the packed congregation gripped by the awe of the moment. Sweet clouds of incense rose around the figure of the priest and for a moment it all seemed remote, like a glimpse into Avea's hidden past, until one recognised the solemn face of Don Anastasio and understood that this was here and now, and that the keening of the relatives was no distant ritual chant but the expression of present human anguish. Old Oreste was dead.

'Receive our brother Oreste in the glory of your Son, who is Lord for ever and ever.'

At the end they extinguished the candles that stood at each corner of the catafalque. Threads of smoke rose up towards the vaulting like the first smoke from a funeral pyre. Old Oreste was dead, and part of the village with him.

As the coffin bearers hoisted their load on to their shoulders, the deacon made his pounce on the processional cross. There was a brief, tense struggle between him and Renzo on the altar steps. No one else made any move. Finally Renzo grabbed the staff away and walked down to take his place at the front of the procession, leaving the deacon empty-handed.

'I am the resurrection and the life, says the Lord.'

The coffin moved forward with Renzo at the head. The deacon followed, scowling. No one had turned a hair or batted an eyelid, but for a moment death had indeed been swallowed up in victory. At the head of the procession Renzo's face was impassive.

So they buried Oreste in the village cemetery where we had gone with him before the olive picking, where we had looked at the indistinct, monochrome faces of his and the village's past. And now he too has a face mounted on a slab of marble, not the Oreste we knew but the face of a younger man just returned from his own ten-year war, slightly drawn, solemn, in stiff collar and tie, photographed for some half-forgotten family occasion. Presumably that was how Lucia wished to remember him. But why not remember him as we knew him, with his awful bowed legs and his broken teeth and his broad grin despite it all and his arthritic hands pouring yet another glass of the wine in which the fruit flies floated like sacrificial victims?

'*Vino genuino*. The flies show it! No chemicals.'

Oreste's death seemed emblematic of the changes in the village. A way of life was passing. There was now scaffolding in the alleys of the *centro storico* and one day we found that the first house we had lived in had been transformed into an artist's gallery. Nearby a ceramic shop opened up selling 'traditional Avese ware'. The Osteria del Re discovered that it had a menu; the Bar Rasenna even started a Saturday night disco in its basement.

Of course all this was only to be expected. In a sense merely to have observed the place as it was is to take part in the change, and to suggest that things should not change is absurd. The Aveani are better off now than they have ever been. They are selling up the old ruins in the *centro storico* and building smart new places on the next hill. They have proper bathrooms instead of those little cabins built out on a balcony over the street. They have space. They do not have damp. And the houses they have left behind are being saved from the decay which at one time seemed inevitable. But remember the words of Tancredi, not the Tancredi of the Osteria del Re, but the Tancredi of *Il Gattopardo*: '*Se vogliamo che tutto rimanga come è, bisogna che tutto cambi.*' If we want everything to stay as it is, everything must change. Italians have an almost infinite capacity for absorbing change. It is both a virtue and a curse.

# Epilogue

Our own search for a house finally took us to another *paese* some twenty minutes drive away from Avea. The *centro storico* of this village is piled onto a promontory which juts out into a wide, volcanic lake. It is every bit as old and far more beautiful than Avea. There is a church at the very summit of the promontory and an ancient Orsini castle beside the main gate and fishermen's cottages clustered along the shore. But the house we had found was modern. There would be no restoration, no reconstruction, no loving preservation of an ancient building – but no leaking roofs and no battle with death watch beetle and dry rot, either.

'We're moving,' we told Pippo and Grazia. 'We have decided to buy a house, so we're giving our notice.'

They nodded thoughtfully. Three months was the legal notice. Three months was the advance rent we had paid as a deposit – three months at the old rate, of course. We smiled and nodded at one another politely over the coffee cups and did rapid mental arithmetic.

'When are you going?' Pippo asked. 'Because there's someone who needs an apartment urgently . . .' He gave the impression of being a great philanthropist.

I shrugged. 'The place is ready. We can move in almost immediately.'

'*Bene*.' He nodded in his imponderable way, the same gesture we had first seen in the scented shadows of the flower shop in the *centro storico*. 'Better to have a place of your own.'

So we left Avea. There were farewells to make, but we were foreigners, birds of passage. *Forestieri* come and *forestieri* go.

It is the way of the world. Grazia shed tears over the baby; Pippo rowed with us about the deposit; we promised to return as soon as possible. We left in the rain, with water glistening on the roof tiles and shining on the basalt setts of the old village. We left it to its own future and our past, and over the years it has been burnished by memory into something more than it really is, which is just one village amongst many in central Italy – nothing special, no store of treasures, no relic of great and stirring events, merely a place where people live and have lived from time – litterally – immemorial; but a place which welcomed us with an instinctive warmth and let us go as we pleased. One could not wish for anything better.

And what are we to it? An entry in some dusty ledger in the archives of the *comune* I suppose, and an entry in the register of baptisms in the parish church of San Lorenzo. A mere blinking of an eye.

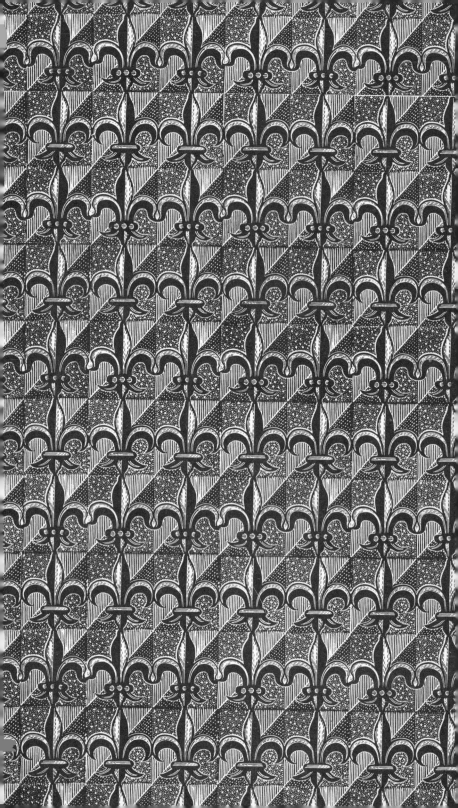